TRUE TALES OF MOTHERS AND FATHERS RUNNING AMOK

- Sandy O., now 38, whose mother sends her monthly packages of clipped-out newspaper photos showing singularly unattractive brides . . . and under each one is painstakingly printed: "If this woman can find a husband, why can't *you?*"
- Roger J., who at 12 years old got his penis caught in his zipper. But the real pain came when his mom laughed hysterically every time she told the story for years afterward.
- Carmen G., who landed a job as a young reporter on the police beat and then had his tough-guy image ruined when his mother called the editor and the cops because he was late coming home.
- Mary Jo B., who on the way to school would lie down on the backseat of the car because her hypochondriac father insisted on wearing a crash helmet even though he only drove 15 miles an hour.

PARENTS FROM HELL

Judith Newman is a journalist who has been published in *Mirabella, Cosmopolitan,* the *New York Times,* and other periodicals. She is also the author of *Tell Me Another One: A Woman's Guide to Men's Classic Lines.*

PARENTS FROM HELL

UNEXPURGATED TALES OF GOOD INTENTIONS GONE AWRY

JUDITH NEWMAN

A PLUME BOOK

PLUME
Published by the Penguin Group
Penguin Books USA Inc., 375 Hudson Street,
New York, New York, 10014, U.S.A.
Penguin Books Ltd, 27 Wrights Lane,
London W8 5TZ, England
Penguin Books Australia Ltd, Ringwood,
Victoria, Australia
Penguin Books Canada Ltd, 10 Alcorn Avenue,
Toronto, Ontario, Canada M4V 3B2
Penguin Books (N.Z.) Ltd, 182–190 Wairau Road,
Auckland 10, New Zealand

Penguin Books Ltd, Registered Offices:
Harmondsworth, Middlesex, England

First published by Plume, an imprint of Dutton Signet, a division
of Penguin Books USA Inc.

First Printing, May, 1995
10 9 8 7 6 5 4 3 2 1

The chapter "So Why Aren't You Married Yet?" first appeared in *Mademoiselle*.

Ⓟ REGISTERED TRADEMARK—MARCA REGISTRADA

LIBRARY OF CONGRESS CATALOGING-IN-PUBLICATION DATA:
Newman, Judith.
  Parents from hell : unexpurgated tales of good intentions / Judith Newman.
    p. cm.
  ISBN 0-452-27234-3
  1. Parents—Humor. I. Title
PN6231.P2N49 1995
818'.5402—dc20   94-43447
                                                          CIP

Printed in the United States of America
Set in Sabon
Designed by Leonard Telesca

BOOKS ARE AVAILABLE AT QUANTITY DISCOUNTS WHEN USED TO PROMOTE PRODUCTS OR
SERVICES. FOR INFORMATION PLEASE WRITE TO PREMIUM MARKETING DIVISION,
PENGUIN BOOKS USA INC., 375 HUDSON STREET, NEW YORK, NEW YORK 10014.

To My Parents
(Can you imagine what
would happen to me if
I didn't dedicate
this book to them?)

The first half of our lives is ruined by our parents
and the last half by our children.

—Clarence Darrow

Table of Contents

* * * *

Table of Contents

Introduction

* * * *

You arrive in this world a lovely package of charm, good-will, and self-esteem. You are perfect, and you know it. A few years later, you are eating worms to gain your friends' approval. Several years after that, you belong to five 12-step programs and you're wondering if that last tattoo was a wise decision. You make your first appearance on *Oprah*. She asks you back.

What happened?

Let me tell you what happened: Parents.

Parents from Hell is a collection of stories from friends, family, acquaintances, and total strangers I worked up the nerve to ask about the memorable, endearing, sometimes outrageous things mom and dad have done in the name of love.

This book is not about abusive parents, or neglecting parents, or parents who in any way resemble Leona Helmsley. We are not here to discuss your inner or outer child, or to figure out how, despite years of psychotherapy, you continue to get involved with men who model their love lives on Caligula's. This is a book about *loving* parents who, with the best of intentions, have made you into the demented individual you are today.

Like many children growing up in the sixties and seventies, television became my gauge for what was desirable in parental behavior, and what was not. Why didn't *my* father wear those cozy patches on his jackets, like Robert Young in *Father Knows Best*? When my friends came over to the house, why couldn't *my* mother whip up batches of chocolate chip cookies the way Donna Reed did when her kids' friends came over? And why was I terrified to bring my friends over to my house in the first place? Well, unlike my mother, Donna Reed didn't sit down with her kids' friends and ask them how much money their parents made.

Fail to fully comprehend the yawning chasm between television parents and your parents? Try this: a side-by-side comparison of *The Brady Bunch*'s Mike Brady and your dad.

When Mike Brady asks Jan: How are you feeling?
He means: How are you feeling?

When your *dad asks you:* How are you feeling?
He means: What's wrong with you? Your face is so red, you look like you're about to have a seizure. Either that, or you're pregnant.

The inspiration for *Parents From Hell* came rather easily. I was sitting at home one morning, waiting for my father's daily 7:45 A.M. phone call (another of those little habits I've never been able to break him of, like giving me his latest prostate update and threatening every other week to cut me out of his will). In the course of the conversation, he asked nonchalantly, "Have you gotten any interesting phone calls lately?" I ignored this question, since my father tends to believe that because I'm a journalist I'm on a first-name basis with every famous person in the country when, in fact, I can't get second-string publicists to return my phone calls.

Several days passed, and Dad kept repeating his question: "Any interesting phone calls?" Finally, after he posed this question for the fifth time, I demanded an explanation.

Unbeknownst to me, my father had been answering personals ads on my behalf. He'd thumb through, say, the *Jewish Weekly*, and spot an ad that began: "Handsome doctor, 38, seeks observant woman. . . ." Never mind that my idea of "observant" is putting a Star of David atop the Christmas tree; never mind, even, *that I'm about to marry someone else* (someone my father disapproves of, which puts him in the same boat as the three hundred other men I've brought home over the last fifteen years). Without saying a word to me, my father had Xeroxed some magazine articles I'd written, and enclosed a note to the gentlemen in the ads that began: "I'm Judith Newman's father, and although she's not the kind of girl who answers personals, she really needs to find a decent man for once in her life. . . ." He then enclosed my phone number *and* address, so in case the doctor in question turned out to be Hannibal Lecter, the man would have no trouble beating a hasty path to my door.

Parents from Hell. Can't live with 'em, can't live . . . with 'em.

(When I told my mother I was working on this book, her

response was, "Will it embarrass me as much as your last one? Oh, well. Maybe it will sell better.")

Parents From Hell is divided into chapters that reflect the glorious milestones of human development: birth, weddings, graduations, humiliating religious rituals, and so forth. Some of the subjects appear in chronological order, but this is purely accidental. Just like your brother who's ten years younger than you.

Parents From Hell is for everyone who has parents, which leaves out Adam and Eve and that French kid who was raised by wolves. With all the very legitimate, very important books for sexually abused children and children of alcoholics, there really isn't anything available for garden-variety neurotics with decent parents who just did weird things—in other words, most of us. This is a book for men and women who can laugh at themselves and their childhoods. It's a book people can give to friends and spouses—and maybe even to mom and dad.

Remember: Your parents only want what's best for you. But if this is their idea of "Best," what do they think of as "Worst"?

"My Kid's Better Than Your Kid"
Parenting as a Competitive Sport

"You should've seen her," my father cackled to my mother. "They were eating her dust." And so began a life in the Baby I.Q. Sweepstakes: At nine months, my father was showing people how I could identify all the parts of my body; at two years, I was singing the alphabet to annoyed mothers in the local playground (who, by this time, knew enough to run when they saw my father coming); by three, I was reciting the Pledge of Allegiance to strangers he would stop on the street. So what if I was too fat to run and too dangerously antisocial to tolerate another child's company for more than two minutes? Hey, I could read every single one of the flash cards my parents had been sticking in my face since I was six months old.

Both fiercely competitive and pathologically defensive (in case any other rug rat one-ups their own), Proud Parents are a dangerous species of beast: They know their kid is the greatest, because, after all, isn't it their *blood coursing through that child's veins?*

Candidates for the Proud Parent Hall of Fame: Teri Shields (Brooke Shields's mother), Joan Crawford in Mildred Pierce—*and that cheerleader's mom in Texas.*

*   *   *   *

It was another typical faculty picnic my father had dragged us kids to. (He was on the faculty of this Virginia woman's college for simpering Southern belles.) The father/professors, all segregated by department, were in one corner of the field, earnestly talking shop; the women were in another corner, getting soused and commiserating with one another on the woes of being faculty wives. The kids were left to their own devices. Normally, the most outrageous thing we could think up to do was to drop chunks of dry ice onto charcoal and watch the clouds of steam, or force the littlest kids to sit on blocks of the dry ice until they started to cry.

But this time around I had an infinitely more interesting project planned. I had talked a girl I lusted after—the daughter of the man who was my father's archenemy in his department—into making out with me in this tree house somebody had built nearby.

We were really going at it, and I had just about gotten her bra undone, when I managed to roll both of us out of the tree house, onto the ground. Fortunately for her, she landed on top of me, and I broke her fall. Unfortunately for me, I cracked several ribs and an arm, and I sprained the muscles in my back.

What happened afterward was kind of hazy, but I still remember waiting for the ambulance while my father and her father hurled insults at each other. The rest of the faculty looked on in that mock-innocent "don't-blame-us-*we're*-not-the-vulgarians" way academics have. The insults had a distinctly college English-department flair: I seem to recall my father calling the girl I was with "a succubus" and her father saying he always knew I was a "wretched little Portnoy." My father took this as an anti-Semitic slur (which, in that little Virginia town, it probably was), and the last thing I saw before they took me away in the ambulance was my little tweedy father and this even runtier guy rolling on the ground.

—Tom D., 35, history teacher, Atlanta, Georgia

P.S. Sixteen years and many relationships later, this girl and I got married. Our fathers still hate each other's guts.

* * * *

Giving birth, to my mother, was what going to war was for many men: the dramatic high point of her life. When I was about ten and had girlfriends over to the house, she used to regale them with graphic descriptions of The Birth, the central theme being how much pain she had to endure in order that I might live. No matter what the conversation was, my mother always worked it around to this thought: "You know, being a woman is not easy." As soon as I heard those words, I knew what was coming: the difficulties of conception ("It took my husband six years . . ."—always with the implication that Dad's sperm weren't up to the task); the exhausting nine-and-a-half months; my lateness ("Joan's never been on time"); the water breaking; the thirty-seven hours of labor; the agony . . . At some point in this lecture, she would usually offer to show my friends her cesarean scar. Clearly there was not a woman on earth who had suffered so much for such an ungrateful daughter.

Thank God I was born before videos became popular; otherwise I'm sure she would be setting up weekly screenings for strangers.

—Joan N., 32, journalist, New York, New York

✳   ✳   ✳   ✳

My mother loved Halloween, and she was determined to be the best Halloween mom in the neighborhood. Every year she'd go all out to be a witch . . . like, she'd cut hairs off her head and paste them into fake moles all over her face. Then she'd wait in the bushes and jump out and ambush kids who were walking up the driveway to our house. She scared one kid so much he peed in his pants.

Mother played her role so convincingly that, after a few years, there was this myth in the neighborhood that she *was* a witch. I still remember coming home crying after getting into a fight with this one girl, who was telling everyone she saw my mom flying over our school on her broom.

—Laurie L., 25, set designer, Austin, Texas

✳   ✳   ✳   ✳

In third grade, I was assigned to write a report on George Washington. I researched it carefully and spent a whole day writing it; I was very proud of my work. Then my mother read it and decided it wasn't up to her standards. So she rewrote it and made me copy in my own handwriting what she'd written. Then she made this elaborate cover for it out of red construction paper, with a red, white, and blue axe with a circle of thirteen stars on it. Then she made me turn it in as my work.

Needless to say, my parents got called in for a talk with the teacher, because Mrs. DeSatos was sharp enough to recognize the difference in the artwork of a third-grader and a professional graphic designer.

—Ben, 19, college student, Chicago, Illinois

*   *   *   *

My friend Shelly was neither the most gorgeous girl nor the best student in the world, but her mother had dreams for her. Big dreams. First of all, she was determined her daughter would grow up to marry a wealthy man, and to do that she needed "class." When we were all in fifth grade, her mom started an etiquette school in her home and hired this woman—who was, I'm convinced, the evil twin of Mrs. Howell on *Gilligan's Island*—to teach us things such as where to place the fish fork on a table setting. We were ten; our mothers were lucky if we remembered even to *use* cutlery. Still, I went to the first session. We had cookies, and that's why I was there; there was no incentive after that first meeting, because there was no food.

Anyway, as we got older, Shelly's mom's plans for her daughter got bigger. Throughout junior high and high school, her mom did virtually all her homework. She was determined her daughter should be in accelerated classes. Shelly used to complain to me about this at first—but as time went on, I guess she thought, *Why bother?*

Life was okay for Shelly until S.A.T. time rolled around. She knew she should never have agreed to her mother's idea, but by that time I guess Shelly didn't have a whole lot of confidence in herself.

Her mother, who was thirty-nine at the time, got dressed in Shelly's clothes and turned up for the exam.

Let's just say things didn't work out. She got caught, Shelly got caught, and the story made all the papers. But things didn't turn out so badly. Shelly left home, worked for a few years, and eventually went back to school. She got her degree, got married to a great (but pretty poor) guy, and proceeded to have five kids in a row, one more adorable than the other.

I think she was pleased to find something she could do *really* well, without her mother's help.

—Ellie C., 30, sales rep, Glen Coe, Illinois

* * * *

I was thirteen years old, sitting at home one day, and bored. So I decided to make a dry-ice bomb. This consists of ground-up dry ice and hot water. You seal the container (in this case a two-liter soda bottle), and the carbon dioxide gets enough force to break through.

At the time, I was having some problems at school. Consequently, on this Sunday afternoon while I was outside making the bomb, my father was on the phone with my school principal, trying to get me off the hook for a variety of disturbances I had been causing.

I had never made this type of bomb before, so I didn't know what to expect. I poured in the hot water, sealed the cap, and waited. Nothing happened, so I went inside to wait and then decided to eavesdrop on my father as he talked to the principal.

The next thing I knew, there was this huge boom that literally shook the ground. My dad didn't know what I was doing, so he had to hang up on my principal to make sure I was still alive. After Dad discovered the neck of the bottle had lodged itself two inches into the side of the house, I was yelled at and given a long lecture about safety.

But this is the reason I love my father: Right after the bomb blew, he called the principal back and told him that if his son is smart enough to know how to make bombs, he should be put into more advanced classes in school. My father convinced the principal that my "attitude" problem resulted from boredom, and they put me in an advanced class.

And it was true: I wasn't a juvenile delinquent by preference. I was obnoxious because I was bored out of my mind.

These days I teach high-school physics.

—Boris A., 31, teacher, Minneapolis, Minnesota

❋ ❋ ❋ ❋

Some might consider it endearing that my parents saved—and displayed—every straight-A report card, horseback riding ribbon, and tennis trophy I ever won, but by the time I was in high school, their awards mania was getting out of hand. If you make a big deal out of *every* little thing that happens in your child's life, the message the child gets isn't, "We think you're swell." It's, "Look at this! Our expectations for you are so low, we're amazed you're even smart enough to win a Girl Scout compass-reading badge!" After a while, I was afraid to mention anything good that happened to me, because however slight it was, my parents would want physical evidence of it to frame or display. Friends who came over referred to our house as The Shrine.

In the years that have passed, I've never quite been able to make them understand how I feel on this issue—which is why I'm now thirty-four, but anyone who comes to their house and doesn't know better thinks they have a somewhat dim seventeen-year-old living with them. They still have all my college acceptance letters framed and proudly displayed in the kitchen.

—Katherine C., 34, ophthalmologist, Rochester, New York

* * * *

Of course, I don't remember this personally, but my father told me about it years later. I was one of those generically cute, blond, blue-eyed babies that advertisers love so much, so when I was about nine months old my mother decided to start my career in show biz. Problem was, I may have been cute, but I had the personality of a tiny Dexedrine-addled sociopath—and in order for a baby to make it in commercials, he or she has to be extremely *mellow.*

My mother refused to accept this fact of life. Instead, she made it her business to disconcert the other mothers who took their babies on auditions, in the hope that all those jangled nerves would tell on the babies. Mom was arsenic with a smile. One time, she walked up to the mother of an adorable, megaplump carrot-top and said to the mother, "Isn't it ironic that the very qualities that make her so cute today are the ones that are going to plague her for the rest of her life?"

My showbiz days were, shall we say, numbered.

—Rebecca P., 23, computer programmer, Los Angeles, California

* * * *

Being a woman in medical school forty years ago was quite an anomaly, and a lot of my fellow students gave me a hard time. But there's one in particular I'll always remember. The first day of school, Paul Frando blocked my path as I was leaving a class and announced, "I don't believe in women doctors." He then went on to explain why, at great length, women were inappropriate in the workplace, ultimately injuring not only themselves but the fabric of the American family. Pompous and obnoxious as he was, he was also very handsome, and women fawned all over him. At one point he was kicked out of school for jumping rope with the intestines of one of the cadavers. But his father, who was a famous cardiologist, got him reinstated.

Anyway, many years passed. I'd heard Paul got married. Then he got divorced, then remarried, then divorced again. Finally, when we were both about fifty, I ran into him at a medical convention. He was as gorgeous as ever—and, I assumed, as arrogant. He had just married for the third time and now had his first children—beautiful twin daughters. He showed me pictures and talked about his kids endlessly. Finally, I couldn't resist asking: "What do you plan to tell your daughters about working women?"

"Which one?" he snapped back. "The doctor or the lawyer?"

—Rachel P., 65, physician, Scarsdale, New York

∗　∗　∗　∗

Birds & Bees
(or How We Learn What Sick, Repellent Monsters Our Parents Are Behind Closed Doors)

Remember the day you found out what sex was—and how, in order for you to come into the world, your parents had to do it?

I was so mortified by this concept I decided that, in fact, these people I called Mom and Dad couldn't be my parents; clearly, they were imposters who had swooped down in the middle of the night and taken the place of my real parents, who were being held hostage by some kindly, fun-loving extraterrestrials. What pranksters those aliens can be! Anyway, I began referring to the people I lived with as Mr. and Mrs. Newman, refusing to explain why.

Fortunately, sometime later I learned about parthenogenesis, and since this was obviously the method of my conception, I'm able to call them Mom and Dad again.

* * * *

One day, when I was in third grade, my friend Debbie and I were having a discussion about where babies came from. She knew, and I didn't. She started to tell me, and then she stopped. I begged and begged, but she wouldn't deal the dirt. Finally we struck a bargain: If I couldn't find out from my own mother, Debbie'd tell me all about it the next day.

So I flew home and demanded my mother tell me where babies come from. Well, my mother didn't want to answer, but then again, she didn't want to *not* answer. Being a fairly precocious—and dramatic—child, I threatened her: *"If you don't tell me, right now, I will learn it on the streets!"*

Finally she relented, giving me this vague, cryptic description. Somehow, all I knew at the end of it was that the vagina was implicated. "A man touches your vagina," she said.

"With his hand?" I asked.

"Well, not his hand," she answered.

And that's all she would say.

But I was so grossed out by the whole thing—a vagina, a hand, a man being involved in any way with the whole proceeding—I didn't go back and ask my friend Debbie for details. In fact, I didn't ask anyone else about the subject for another year.

Fast-forward to fifth grade. I had pretty much figured out the details of The Act for myself. I was really into reading trashy novels, and at the time I was engrossed with Irving Wallace's book *The Word*. Suddenly, I was startled by this one scene: The hero and heroine go into the shower, soap each other up, rinse off, and *the woman puts the man's penis in her mouth.*

Well, here was a piece of news. Immediately I rushed off to my grandmother who lived with us, and I read her this part from the chapter (in Spanish—my family is Cuban). Then I paused, waiting for an explanation.

"I have no idea what you're talking about," she replied.

Dissatisfied, I hunted down my mother, who was feeding the chickens in the backyard. I read the passage to her.

"Well, what do you want to know?" she asks.

"Is it true?" I want to know. "Do people do this?"

"Well . . . yes, they do."

This was good, but not quite good enough. "Do *you* do this?"

Mom was never a good liar. "Well . . . yes. Sometimes. Not often."

Now I was pleased. If my mother does it, obviously it really happens—and it can't be a bad thing. I decided to go back to my grandmother with the good news.

Strangely enough, my grandmother was much less pleased than I was. I was puzzled. We dropped the subject.

From that day onward, for as long as she lived with us, my grandmother kept two sets of silverware separate from the rest—for me and her—wrapped in plastic *and stored in the oven*. So no one could possibly use them by mistake.

—Nikki G., 33, lawyer, San Francisco, California

✳   ✳   ✳   ✳

I come from the healthiest terminal family in the world. They are always at death's door. My mother gets cancer, and it goes into complete remission; my father's had four heart attacks—and still, like the Energizer bunny, he keeps going and going and going. Which reminds me of how they told me about sex.

My mother was working as the school librarian for a

while. I was in fourth grade, and a book I was reading mentioned wet dreams. I just didn't get it: The character in this book sort of wet the bed, but then again, it was okay. And it had something to do with sex.

So I walked into the teacher's lounge and asked, "Mom, when am I going to start getting wet dreams?"

She told me to hush up, and she'd tell me later. I couldn't wait till I got home.

That night, Mom sat me down on the loveseat in our living room and explained everything to me, from DNA and chromosomes to the baby emerging from the uterus. The explanation went on for hours. It was so complicated, so convoluted . . . somehow she left me with the distinct impression that intercourse was a medical procedure that had to be performed by a team of doctors. *And it had something to do with being ill.*

I spent the next six months masturbating to the idea of hospitals. This was how I thought you did sex: You and the girl would check into a room at the hospital, where you'd both get undressed behind changing curtains. A nurse would be waiting for you and would lead you to bed. Then a doctor would appear, to help you with the penile insertion.

Then somehow, in porno-movie fashion, the nurse got involved. The whole thing was tied up with microscopes, needles, lab coats . . . to this day, a Bunsen burner does strange things for me.

—Jim A., 43, magazine editor, New York, New York

✳   ✳   ✳   ✳

When I was fifteen, I went to Phillips Academy for the summer session. My father thought he was spending his money wisely, when in fact I spent all my time smoking hash and sitting in the bird sanctuary, staring into space.

The main reason they sent me to prep school was to get me away from my boyfriend, whom they hated. Ronnie had bright red hair, droopy drawers, and the intelligence of an Irish setter. But over the summer, I had seen the musical *Hair*—and that song "16-Year-Old Virgin" really upset me. I thought it was time to get rid of my virginity, so whenever I wasn't stoned I was in the Andover library researching birth-control methods and plotting to give myself to Ronnie when I returned. I promised my best friend at prep school that when I went back and did the deed, I'd report to her.

So, birth-control pills in hand, I returned home in the fall and—well, actually I got cold feet. I kept postponing and postponing, until Ronnie practically raped me in the backseat of his car. The deed done, I wrote my girlfriend a letter describing every detail. I later found out she never received it, because my father had intercepted it.

Without discussing it with me first, my father called Ronnie's father to give him the bad news. I eavesdropped on the conversation from the other room. My father was infuriated by Ronnie's father's response, which was, "I told him it was okay, as long as he didn't get caught."

From that day on, my father would only allow me to go out with boys who were not Ronnie. So Ronnie and I had a little system: He'd get one of his friends to pick me up at my house, and we'd walk off, arm in arm—until the point where the designated date would take me to my greasy little swain. It was all very *West Side Story,* I thought. We went together for years. The guy was such a moron, I'm sure I wouldn't have gone out with him longer than a couple of months if my father hadn't fanned the flames by hating him so much.

—Cecilia, 39, biologist, Roanoke, Virginia

*   *   *   *

I have to say that despite my parents' repressed Catholic upbringing—or maybe because of it—they were determined for me to understand the facts of life. So for my seventh birthday I got a copy of *How Babies Are Made,* an illustrated book from Time/Life. I remember it so vividly. It was a lavender book with baby-blue trimming; it started out by explaining sex in the plant kingdom, worked its way from ferns to chickens, dogs, horses, and then finally mommy and daddy in bed. Even though Mom and Dad went out of the way to buy me this book, they didn't want to actually discuss it. They told me if I had any questions, I could discuss them with the nurse at school. Naturally, I didn't dare.

I waited until sixth grade, where we were shown a sex-ed film; the only thing I remember were these animated characters, Sammy Sperm and Edith Egg. Sammy was wearing a little top hat and tails and a boutonniere, and Edith was decked out in a wedding gown, complete with veil and train. They marched down the aisle together.

So even though I had learned how things really worked in sex-ed, I always preferred to think there was a little wedding reception going on in my uterus.

—Maryanne C., 27, news reporter, St. Louis, Missouri

*   *   *   *

Mom was taking my older brother and me to school, and
to break the silence, my brother asks, "Mom, what's *fuck*?"

Without missing a beat, Mom says, "Well, *fuck* is a bad
word for a good thing. Like, you know, if you have to go to
the bathroom at school, you don't raise your hand and say,
'Excuse me, I have to take a shit.' Shitting and fucking are
both good things to do; they're just not the best words to
use."

This is the explanation I want to give to *my* kids someday.

—Tracy L., 26, waitress, Bowdoin, Maine

✳ ✳ ✳ ✳

I was so socially retarded, I never thought to ask my parents *anything* about sex until I was about twelve. But when
I said something like, "Where do babies come from?" it
was as if my mother had been rehearsing for this moment
for the last twenty years. She dashed to her closet and pro-
duced this three-dimensional replica of a woman's repro-
ductive system she must have bought at a medical supply
store. Then, she whipped out several pages of notes and
proceeded to explain the whole process in excruciating detail: "In the lower abdomen on each side of the uterus
there is an ovary. About every four weeks during a woman's fertile years, several eggs ripen in the ovaries in little
sacs called follicles. The follicles send a hormone called es-
trogen into the blood, which causes the cervix . . ." And on
and on and *on*.

After about an hour, I stopped her. In retrospect, I think
I would have been better off with, "When two people love
each other, they get married and do things only married

people can do that allow them to have babies." Either that, or something about a stork.

—Joan N., 32, journalist, New York, New York

* * * *

Growing up in a very religious family, my mother had a hard time talking to me about sex. Here was her one piece of advice: She waited till the spring of my senior year in high school, held my hands, looked deeply into my eyes, and said, "If you do more than kiss, it is a sin." Needless to say, I'd already done more than that. I left the house and went straight to confession.

—Marian, 40, homemaker, Detroit, Michigan

* * * *

I've known I was a lesbian since I was a little kid. Three years ago my mother told me she could not accept my "life-style" but still loved me. Two months ago she moved in with her female lover. Eight months ago she slept with a woman for the first time. Six months before that, I slept with the same woman. (Are you following this?) My mom has gone from 0-to-dyke in six months.

Watch for us on *Geraldo* next season.

—Margaret, 25, Vancouver, Canada

* * * *

When I was thirteen and got my first period, my mother was thrilled. . . . the Threshold of Womanhood, and all that. She took me to the drugstore to buy some pads. As we were standing in the aisle looking at the different types, she decided to ask a woman standing nearby what was the best brand to use, as it was her daughter's first time—then she pointed at me and said, "Right, honey?" The woman mumbled something and took off. It then became my mother's quest: She polled every woman she ran into, including the checkout girl, as to what she used and why. And she never forgot to tell them the reason she was asking. I just kept trying to get lost in the store; I remember stationing myself in the dental hygiene department, trying to appear as if the most fascinating thing I'd ever seen was a tube of toothpaste.

—Jean, 23, actress, Brooklyn, New York

* * * *

I'll never forget the look on Mom's face when, at age twelve, I wandered in and asked, "What's venereal disease?" (I think I was reading *1984* or *Brave New World* at the time.) Her response: "Ask your father."

My father (who undoubtedly delivered this wisdom while he was shaving in the bathroom—that's where we had all our father-son talks), said, cryptically, "Don't worry. It's something you can catch only when you're a man." I assumed, therefore, that it was something you got when you cut yourself shaving, since that's what men did that I couldn't do. For a while after that, I sat around and thought about nicking myself with a razor and getting a venereal disease—thus proving to my parents, once and for all, that I was grown-up.

—Bradley, 28, travel agent, Boston, Massachusetts

* * * *

This was the sum total of our sex talk: When I was thirteen, my mother turned to me and said, "Remember, boys are going to want to touch you now—but not below the waist."

—Carey L., 43, lawyer, New York, New York

* * * *

When we were young and used to come home from school with those "new words" that every parent hopes their children won't pick up, Mom always dealt with the situation by explaining *exactly* what the word meant and chased it with, "Now is that really what you meant to say?" Since the mental pictures were horrifying beyond belief, we never picked up the words for casual use.

—Emma P., 38, graphic designer, Newport, Rhode Island

* * * *

When I was thirty, I decided to come out to my parents; I was sure it was going to be one of the most traumatic moments of my life, but I had to do it. Imagine my surprise when my father told me he knew I was a lesbian years ago, because he used to eavesdrop on my conversations with my first lover. As soon as he told me this, I began to blast him for his lack of respect for my privacy. Then he added, rather sheepishly, that actually he'd hoped he'd find the conversation titillating, but he gave up listening because they were so *boring*.

So what's worse—a parent who spies on you, or one who finds your lesbian love life dull?

—Brenda, 36, sportswear designer, New York, New York

* * * *

When I was in high school, we lived in a two-story house. One day as I was sitting downstairs with my new boyfriend, smooching, my mom walked in on us. Believe me, there wasn't even a hand straying below the waist in this scenario—but, still, my mom was so shocked she froze in her tracks and fled upstairs. I didn't know what to do . . . and then I heard this muffled yelp. I ran to her: My mother, in her haste, had fallen *up* the stairs and broken her ankle. My boyfriend and I had to drive her to the hospital.

She never mentioned a word about seeing us kiss.

—Rhonda, 30, physical therapist, Taos, New Mexico

✳   ✳   ✳   ✳

I learned about sex from a friend's father, who used the metaphor of the penis as a hypodermic needle through which you "injected" a woman with a baby. For the whole summer, my friend was trying to take his dick off; he thought it sort of unscrewed.

Kids take everything literally. At about the same time, I remember catching my grandfather taking his teeth out. He told me everybody could do that. So of course I spent weeks trying to find the latch in my mouth that would allow me to take my teeth out. My mother would say, "Get your hands out of your mouth," and I'd reply, "Wait, I think I found the hook here."

—Jason G., 40, newspaper editor, Little Rock, Arkansas

✳   ✳   ✳   ✳

Baptisms, Birthdays, and Other Family Rituals That Scarred Us for the Rest of Our Lives

Have you ever noticed how the calmest, brightest, most sophisticated person you know—the one who can whip up a perfect plate of angel hair primavera and truffles in minutes, who can rattle off Antonioni's entire oeuvre in chronological order, the one who travels in circles you only dream of— have you ever noticed how this person becomes a sulking eight-year-old at family gatherings?

There is a reason for this: No matter how much of a big shot you are to the rest of the world, no matter how many multimillion-dollar deals you cut or lives you save, your parents know the real you: The dirty, smelly, snotty cheesebrain you were and, in their eyes, will always be. And it's not enough for them to see you this way: They want to make sure you *know that they know.*

Which is why family occasions were invented.

✳   ✳   ✳   ✳

When I left for college, I was a fine, upstanding citizen: an "A" student, a head cheerleader, a member of the Young Republican Club in high school. When I returned for the first holiday break, Thanksgiving of my freshman year, I was smoking clove cigarettes, wearing Indian wraparound skirts over unshaven legs, organizing Take Back the Night marches, and spouting a variety of strongly held opinions on issues I knew nothing about. My parents, needless to say, were none too pleased.

As my aunt and uncle were carving the Thanksgiving turkey, I decided the moment was right: I stood up and delivered a carefully prepared speech about how disgusting Thanksgiving was—a thinly disguised ritual celebrating the slaughter of millions of Native Americans. I denounced white settlers, meat eaters (I was macrobiotic, of course), the near-extermination of the buffalo, the rapaciousness of those involved in real estate (my father was a broker), and anything else I could think of. Then I sat down.

Twenty years have passed. I am now a thirty-nine-year-old woman, about to have a child of my own. But every Thanksgiving, without fail, the meal begins with my father's plea: *"Hey, Joanne, you want to tell us about the Indians again?"*

—Joanne, 39, lawyer, Washington, D. C.

* * * *

My daughter, who just turned one, has all the cognizance of a sea slug, but that didn't stop my mother from insisting we hold a birthday party and invite all the young kids in the neighborhood. I said no, explaining that we could plan the most extravagant party in the world, and to Catherine it would just be an excuse to throw new kinds of food. End of story—or so I thought.

I had gone out for several hours on Catherine's birthday, and came back to find my mother dressed as a clown, my entire house overrun with neighborhood nannies eating Chinese food, and kids hurtling around my kitchen and living room. My mother had bought each kid several party favors, including one bow-and-arrow contraption that turned the most adorable two-year-old into a killing machine. Just as I was trying to prevent half the kids in my neighborhood from becoming cyclopes, I noticed, in the corner of my vision, our resident three-year-old arsonist about to torch my daughter's head.

My mother's response? "You may not *think* the baby remembers her first birthday, but children remember these things."

—Marcelle D., 33, journalist, Hastings-on-Hudson, New York

※   ※   ※   ※

There are periods of time I don't talk to my parents for two or three years at a stretch. The last time was kicked off by this little incident.

I live in New York City, but I go out to Wichita once a month to see my kids; my first wife, who still lives near my parents, and I are in the middle of a custody battle. But things had been pleasant between my parents and me for a few years. While I was out there, my parents suggested: "Why don't you make Thanksgiving dinner here at our house this year? You'll have Thanksgiving with the kids; it'll just be a week early."

This sounded fine, as it enabled me to be with my children from my first marriage for a special occasion and still be with the children from my second marriage on Thanksgiving Day. I'm the chef in the family, so I'd do all the cooking.

So—I'm just leaving to go to the airport on a Thursday night, when I get this phone call from my parents: "Hi, hon! Guess where we are! We're at Kennedy Airport! We're going to Europe for a month!"

I said—"Wait! What about Thanksgiving at your house?" Well, this special opportunity came up, and . . . they hadn't forgotten—they simply hadn't bothered to tell me to make other arrangements.

In the end I had to convince my kids, "Gee! Won't it be fun to have Thanksgiving in a Kansas motel room! We'll watch X-rated movies!"

—George P., 43, editor, New York, New York

✳   ✳   ✳   ✳

Family rituals usually revolve around food—except in my family, the rituals revolve around *no* food. My mother was into the vegan movement—it was sort of the U.K. "take" on Hinduism. George Bernard Shaw was their most famous practitioner, and my mom loved Shaw. Not only did she not believe in eating animal products—for a long time she also didn't believe in cooking anything. I was six years old before I tasted any cooked food. She also felt very strongly that fasting was important for health, so once every six months or so four of us kids had to fast for four or five days. Just *try* to get a seven-year-old to grasp the concept, "Hunger is good for you."

What really scared us was when I had just turned eight

and my mother started reading about the Breatharians—some group of people in the Himalayas who had reportedly learned to exist on air. Weaning food out of your life was an idea that was incredibly appealing to my mother; we just thought she was weird at the time, but in retrospect I think she had a food disorder that she was forcing on all of us.

Luckily my father didn't buy into the Breatharians, or I guess I wouldn't be here to talk about all this. It all seems kind of funny now, although for many years I struggled with anorexia, due in no small part to my mother's ambivalence toward food—and, I guess, nurturing. Every day she would tell us, "If it weren't for you kids, I would have done something with my life."

And today my mother wonders why I don't have any children.

—Francine N., 34, photographer, Houston, Texas

✳   ✳   ✳   ✳

Everyone central to the story has died, so I'm safe telling it. The mothers-in-law both decided they'd come for Christmas. The sniping began on day one. When they ran out of things to criticize about each other (one was too fat, the other too thin), they started in on us. My mother thought my husband drank too much; my husband's mother thought I didn't cook well. She managed to get two zingers in one with that remark, because my mother, who's Italian and very proud of her cooking, had taught me how to cook.

Since the two of them were acting like children, we decided to treat *them* like children. When our kids squabbled, we'd distract them with something to do, so we set these two to making a fruit salad for dinner. (My husband questioned the wisdom of putting them in the same room together with sharp knives.)

Before Mom set about attacking the fruit, I said something terribly provocative like, "I think I'll make dinner."

"*Make* dinner?" my mother-in-law cried. "You don't *make* dinner. You don't *make* the eggs. You don't *make* the milk." She sat back smugly. "You *fix* dinner."

"*Fix* dinner?" my mother bellowed back. "Now it needs to be *fixed*? *Why are you always saying my daughter can't cook?*"

At that point, we had to physically separate them. Since we had quite a few guests coming that year, we managed to sit one of them at the adults' table and one at the kids' table. Even then, the mothers-in-law couldn't refrain from taking a few cheap shots. Hissing within earshot of my husband's mother whenever possible, my mother spent the evening explaining to anyone who'd listen: "Obviously my daughter had to sit me at the children's table, since I'm younger."

—Jennifer, 38, homemaker, Hanover, New Hampshire

✳   ✳   ✳   ✳

Every so often, while my three younger brothers and I were growing up, my mom and dad (but usually my mom) would be overcome with the urge to find a "Fun Thing to Do" for the children.

Now, my parents hung around with people considerably younger than they were, and that meant that their friends' children were younger than everyone but my youngest brother. The older three of us theorized that this is why the Fun Things to Do were geared to kids roughly half our age.

But if we didn't go along and have lots of fun, my mother wouldn't let us forget it: I mean, here she'd planned a Fun Thing to Do for the Whole Family, and we were just a bunch of ingrate slobs, that's all we were, and see if she wore herself out finding More Fun Things to Do *ever* again.

Then, horrifyingly, a couple of months later, her enthusiasm for fun would be rekindled all over again.

The very, very last Fun Thing was the perfect swan song for the whole concept. This happened one winter, when we were living in Minnesota, about one hundred miles south of Minneapolis. Our ages were nineteen, sixteen, thirteen, and nine. My mother saw an ad in the paper for a performance by the Royal Lipizzaner Stallions in Minneapolis, and for reasons known only to herself she decided going to see the horses would be a Fun Thing to Do. So she got on the phone, bought us all tickets, and promoted the hell out of this horse show for about two weeks as a Fun, Fun *Fun* Thing to Do.

The big night (about 16 degrees below zero, with a wind chill factor of minus 30), we all pile into the car and head off on our one-hundred-mile trip. First, of course, we had to live through the usual amount of piddling around, Father tapping his watch in annoyance, and the whining that usually precedes any family trip in which three out of six people don't want to participate; one person (Mother) had no concept of time, and the other (Dad) was only aware that if we didn't leave *right this minute* we were going to miss the whole thing.

Well, we got there, had to pay extra for parking (which really peeved Dad), found our seats way the hell up in the bleachers of this huge sports arena and . . . well, what can you say about two hours of dancing horses, really, after you've driven two hours in arctic temperatures to get there?

(Did I mention that the car heater was on the fritz, and we had to huddle together just to avoid frostbite?)

The horses are supposed to be exquisitely noble and ethereal, so the highlight of the evening was watching the arena staff trying valiantly to whisk away vast quantities of manure before anyone really noticed it was there. And we had all forgotten that my youngest brother, who might at least have gotten some enjoyment out of the whole thing, was allergic to hay; by intermission he was wheezing and asking my dad if he remembered to bring his inhaler.

My older brothers and I started making wisecracks about the show after about ten minutes; after an hour my mother was cringing in her seat. We stuck it out to the end and finished by yelling in unison, "Let's hear it for the shit!" during the final curtain call.

Years later, all I have to do is say the word *Lipizzaner* to my mother, and she'll start to laugh till she cries. I've been meaning to get her a big poster of a dancing white horse ridden by some guy in a Napoleon costume, but I think it might be hazardous to her health.

—Todd L., 34, real-estate broker, Key West, Florida

✳   ✳   ✳   ✳

We begged him. We pleaded. We cajoled. I promised I would go to synagogue every Saturday for the rest of my life if he didn't do it. But my father wanted his day of triumph. At my bat mitzvah, he insisted on singing every last verse of "Sunrise, Sunset" ("Where is the little girl I carried?" etc., etc.)—accompanied by a slide show of my mother giving birth to me.

—Ivy B., 36, speech therapist, Waltham, Massachusetts

* * * *

It was tough growing up Catholic in Indiana. It's not exactly a region of the country known for its seafood; combine this with my mother's brand of cooking, and you had trouble on Fridays' "meatless" evenings.

To my mom, fish was something that came in a rectangular block. It was a slab of frozen cod (not even fish sticks) that one would normally thaw for two hours, separate fillets, and poach. But this was not my mother's cooking method of choice. Her recipe was as follows:

1. Take frozen cod block, wrapped in paper, from freezer, and place on dry cookie sheet.
2. Turn oven to approximately 750 degrees.
3. Insert cookie sheet and cook for twenty minutes or until you can peel the burnt shards of the wrapper off the fish.
4. Reinsert cod block into the oven. You'll know it's done when you can pull the pieces of plastic from between the fillets. You've got it right when the cod has the consistency of a calzone: a hard, crusty shell and a soft, gooey center.

Mom's method of serving was to slice this block diagonally and dish out small bricks of it to each of us.

Fish Block was served with the salad course, which involved taking a cleaver to a head of lettuce and then throwing this, with a few carrots (tops included), into a large bowl, and filling the bowl with water. Then you poured off half of the water and poured in the dressing—because with the water still on, my mother reasoned, the Thousand Island dressing would be incorporated better into all the leaves of lettuce.

Dessert involved the same cooking process as the fish, except with a Sara Lee cheesecake.

The reason my mother was such a bad cook was that my dad was so nice. Every night, for eighteen years, we heard the same thing: "Honey, this is a feast." *My* theory is that she cooked like this just to get a rise out of him—just to see if he dared to say something disparaging, at which point she could turn to him and say, "Why don't *you* cook for a change?" This ploy never worked. In forty years of marriage, he's never said a bad word about a piece of food served to him at home.

—Michael A., 39, train conductor, Dover, Delaware.

* * * *

My father was a local politician, which meant we kids saw very little of him—so when he *did* take us out, we were all thrilled. In retrospect, I'm not sure why—because this is what he'd do, every Sunday, during our afternoon drive: He'd drive us over to the local orphanage and say solemnly, "This is where you'll all end up if you don't behave." We'd all laugh at first—but as time went on, the threat had a bit of weight, because eventually he became a family court judge.

—Pauline F., 55, physician, New Orleans, Louisiana

* * * *

My mother gets a little giddy around Halloween. She loves the holiday so much, I was always scared she would insist on getting dressed up and coming trick-or-treating with us kids. Every year she threatened. We had to buy her off with some of our candy.

One year Mom and I were at the mall, shopping for my costume. I was twelve or so, and I was beginning to feel a little old for this sort of thing—but I hated to disappoint Mom. She was so happy. Anyway, we were in the parking garage elevator with another mom and son who were arguing over what floor they left the car on. It was the day before Halloween. My mother noticed the boy's mother was clutching a rumpled paper bag; protruding out of it was a plastic hand. In her usual jovial way, Mom remarked, "I see there's a hand sticking out of your bag." The woman, who was just about to get off the elevator, mumbled, "Yes, there is." Whereupon Mom replied, "Well, what's your son going to be this year? Captain Hook? My son was Hook a few years ago, and . . ."

As this exchange was going on, I noticed that there was another thing in the bag that didn't really look like a Halloween costume but more like some sort of custom-molded medical equipment. I tried nudging my Mom, but she was unstoppable: "You know, a few years ago I made Elliot a peg leg, when he was Long John Silver . . ."

Finally the disturbed-looking mother and son got off the elevator. When Mom continued speculating about his Halloween costume—despite the fact this boy was, oh, about 18—I suggested an alternative explanation for the arm: Could it have anything to do with the fact that her son had only one arm? Mom blanched. Then she screamed. Then she spent the next twenty-four hours asking me, "You're kidding, right? It's a joke? Please tell me it's a joke. . . ."

—Elliot D., 24, graduate student, Chicago, Illinois

* * * *

Whenever I came home from college, my mother would prepare my favorite meal—grilled lamb chops, home fries, corn, collard greens, blackberry cobbler. Problem is, she's very absentminded, and she was always having to rush out at the last minute because she had forgotten to buy some ingredient.

But this particular time, she was extremely proud of herself; she remembered everything. And I was halfway through dinner (which was delicious), when she suddenly got this troubled look on her face.

"I can't remember. Did I spray the pan I grilled those lambchops in with *Pam* . . . or *Raid?*"

The top of the *Pam* spray was off. But then again, so was the top on the *Raid*.

—David L., 41, architect, Shawnee Mission, Kansas

✳   ✳   ✳   ✳

Nightmare Family Vacations
"Dad, Josh Put a Curse on Me, and He Says That When the Mileage Thing Reaches FIFTY THOUSAND, I'm Going to Blow Up . . ."

Here's my theory: Happy people don't travel. Who would willingly subject themselves to the various terrors of a holiday (tediously hyped Wonders of the World, mystery food, filthy, cramped public transportation, unctuous hotel staff bent on petty larceny, and especially one's fellow tourists)—unless daily life has become so unbearable that anything, *even Cancun, looks better? So, therefore, travelling with the family is some kind of double-dip horror:* You're miserable, and you're taking the main source of your misery with you.

When my mother decided it was time for me to see America, *I was fourteen—just the age when most girls want to spend one month locked in a car with their mothers. So we loaded up the Olds and revved up for what I now think of as "The Summer I Finally Got to Read* Anna Karenina." *I don't remember much of that six-thousand-mile journey, but I do remember sounds occasionally emanating from the front seat: "For Christ's sake, we're passing the Grand Canyon! Look out the window!"*

*   *   *   *

You have to understand, there were eight of us in the family LTD ball-buster station wagon. That meant four in the middle seat, three in the front seat, and one poor sucker with the lawn chairs and cooler in the back—a cooler packed with enough provisions to ensure that if we got stuck in Death Valley we'd survive. There was also the dog, who had to come with us because the one time we tried to leave her with neighbors it was like *The Incredible Journey;* she ran away and tried to find us. Anyway, you get the picture: six kids under fifteen, bare thighs on vinyl seats, large, hairy dog looking for a place to roost, dog claws on thighs, dog snot dripping down the window where she rested her nose.

Riding backward in the backseat was a surefire recipe for vomiting. Every year our parents would be shuffling us kids around, trying us all out in the backseat to see if any of us were vomit-proof. None of us were, and we all suffered from vomit sympathy: As soon as one started—the one riding backward, inevitably—at least a couple more would follow.

In addition to the survival cooler, my mother packed the tinkle can, so we'd never have to stop until we reached our destination. (God forbid we used a gas-station toilet: Sitting on the seat, in my mother's view, was as good as *inviting* gonorrhea into your body. Thanks to this family rule, I developed tremendous thigh muscles.) Now, I'm the only girl in a family of five brothers, so naturally I had to learn to be a camel, because I wasn't about to use the can. Especially with Lawrence, my oldest brother, holding it for all the younger ones, while the can got dangerously full at 60 mph.

During the trip, if the fights reached the point where my father had to intervene, we knew we were doomed—because he never faked a threat. He'd say, "If this doesn't stop, one of you is getting out." Almost always this was enough to quiet us down, but I remember one time my brothers continuing to fight—*and he just dumped the youngest one on the side of a deserted stretch of road and drove away.* We drove just far enough to be out of sight, so my brother had the fear of God put in him, and then my father reversed back down the highway and picked him up. The screeching boy Dad had left behind was gone; what climbed back into our car was a mute.

My father was also famous for his roadside spanks. He'd say, "Get out of the car and pull down your pants—*now.*" This seems so barbaric now, when nobody dares touch their kids, but I have to say in the early sixties, it was pretty effective. The key to spanking, in general, is to make the kid anticipate it. I mean, if one of us did something bad in the morning, and my mother, ever the weenie, said, "You're going to get a spanking when your father gets home," . . . well, you'd really rather be shot in the head than spend a day anticipating his wrath. My youngest brother eventually learned to say, "Look, just spank me now. I don't want to ruin my day thinking about it."

Anyway, back to travelling . . . God forbid we all went to a restaurant together. My father was one of these men who hated drawing attention to himself and his family in public—but how could six kids *not* draw attention to themselves? The simplest meal was a logistical fiasco.

I particularly remember one time, where we were visiting one of those expensive, gimmicky places where the walls are hung with paraphernalia like bales of hay and ploughshares. Everything is geared to taking your money—a kid's fantasyland and a parent's nightmare. Dad immediately started naming the rules, starting with the Forbidden Breadsticks: We weren't allowed to eat them, because they would spoil our expensive dinner.

Meanwhile, sensing a tableful of greedy monsters, the waitress kept arriving with little canapés, shrimps, etc., etc., before the main courses—"Compliments of the house," we were told. We were goggle-eyed. All this bounty before the main dish! We tucked in, as if my parents hadn't bothered to feed us for the duration of the vacation. And Dad couldn't yell, because it was free! "Compliments of the house!"

My brother Jay, who was six, was eating as if this was his last meal. Mom kept telling him to slow down, to no avail. Finally he downed one glass of water too many and *spewed* over the entire table. I wasn't sure whether my father was going to die or kill us first.

The waitress didn't miss a beat: She just grabbed the linen tablecloth and wrapped everything on the table—china, glasses, cutlery—into one big sack and hoisted it away.

"Compliments of Jay," my oldest brother murmured without missing a beat.

And Jay piped up, "Good, now I have room for dessert!"

Dessert is very important to a six-year-old.

You know what? As I write about all this, those trips don't sound like a lot of fun, but we kids always had a *great* time. And we thought our parents were so mean to us, but, in retrospect, they must have been simply out of their minds to undertake these family vacations. I have only two kids, and already I'm semi-dreading our first long car ride/ vacation as a family. How did my parents do it? No wonder my father had a drinking problem.

—Patricia G., 31, elementary-school teacher, Hastings-on-Hudson, New York

* * * *

Whenever Mom travelled, she developed a kind of fashion dementia: She'd see some native design and decide that nothing, *nothing* in the entire world, would look more adorable on me. Since I, as a thirteen-year-old, had about as much fashion sense as Andrea Dworkin, I blithely went along with all the costumes she chose to adorn me with. In the course of one week, I could be Pocahontas (visit to Navaho reservation—beaded headband, suede fringed skirt and vest), Heidi (Switzerland trip—smock, dirndl skirt, embroidered flowers) or an Indian Princess (vacation in New Delhi—she was into the silk sari, but fortunately stopped short of putting the dot on my forehead). I could go on, but suffice it to say that for a thirteen-year-old girl growing up in the largely upper-middle-class Jewish community of Scarsdale, New York, lederhosen are not a good bet, sartorially speaking.

—Joan N., 32, journalist, New York, New York

* * * *

The fact that my father is practically blind in no way diminishes his enthusiasm for photography. He has approximately five thousand pictures taken in thirty countries, and six of them are in focus. Of those six, I think five are pictures of cows in Ireland. However, I'm sure the camera is always in focus—for him.

What's even weirder is that my parents could write a travelogue of the planet, but they never seem to do anything that's interesting to anyone else on earth but them. I'll ask, "Did you see such-and-such a museum?" or "Did you go skiing?" The answer is always, "No." And they'll never quite say what it is they *did* do. At one point, my brothers and I joked that they worked for the KGB.

The worst part about travelling with them, though, was that my father always insisted on driving. (He himself didn't learn until he was thirty-six.) While we were on the road, he'd be driving and planning his college lectures at the same time . . . and suddenly one of us would look over and realize he'd taken his hands off the wheel.

He also insisted on teaching *us* to drive. Consequently, my sister thinks anything concrete is a highway. My brother, after his first year with a license, was known as "The Pedestrian," because he totalled two cars and was banned from driving until college. I won't talk about my own accidents. Let's just say I'm having a little problem getting insurance at the moment.

We are a family of highway menaces. So if you see any of us driving, pull over to the side of the road, get out of your car, and *run!*

—Paul M., 40, carpenter, Newburyport, Massachusetts

✳   ✳   ✳   ✳

Let me try to paint the picture of the hell that is our family vacation. I sit in the back. My father insists on driving. My mother is deaf in her left ear, and my dad mumbles a lot—so all I hear for hours on end is:

"Mmmmmnmnmnhhhhmmm."

"WHAT?"

"Mmmnnhhhmmmmhhm."

"WHAT?"

"Mmmnnnnmhhh."

—Bob S., 17, high-school student, Fresno, California

* * * *

I was two years old and my father was taking me on my first airplane ride. While the plane was still on the ground, I just had to ask, in my piping voice that could be heard by all, "Daddy, do they have potties on airplanes?" Now, forty years later, whenever I meet him at the airport, he can't resist asking me, in a booming voice, "Was the potty okay?" I think this joke began to wear thin when I was in my thirties.

—April M., 42, insurance executive, Boise, Idaho

* * * *

My mom believes in getting the most out of a vacation—the most miles, that is. She was fanatic about those yearly driving vacations. And while in the car, she would pull out her atlas and Mobil Travel Guides and begin planning next year's trip.

One year we went from Chicago to California and back in two and a half weeks. We travelled Route 66 through St. Louis, Tulsa, Amarillo, New Mexico . . . We then went to the Grand Canyon, Hoover Dam, and Las Vegas. From there we travelled to Ventura (to see relatives) and used that as our base to see L.A., Disneyland, San Diego, and Tijuana. We then travelled to San Francisco and Reno; then Salt Lake City, Yellowstone, Denver, somewhere in Nebraska, Cedar Rapids, and finally home.

Since, on a trip like this, San Diego and Montana tend to blur in the mind of an eight-year-old, my mother would head for the nearest souvenir stand wherever we stopped for the night and buy my sister and me a charm in the shape of each state for our charm bracelets. The object was not to actually spend time in the place but *to say we'd been there.*

One of the few unblurred memories I have is, after several hours of driving on I-80 and wondering when we would be getting to Cheyenne, Wyoming, from Yellowstone, my dad complained to my mother that the setting sun was in his eyes. Now, if you look at a map, you will notice that Cheyenne is *east* of Yellowstone, and the sun sets in the *west*. After so many days of driving, my father had made the wrong turn, and no one noticed for *hours.*

—Sharon S., 28, bartender, Los Angeles, California

✻　✻　✻　✻

When taking vacation photos, the viewfinder was simply not a concept my father could grasp. He would just sort of point the camera in the general direction of the object he hoped to photograph. So our vacation pictures consist of lots of photos of my mother's breasts.

—Ann G., 33, lawyer, San Francisco, California

✻　✻　✻　✻

Some people fear death; others fear maiming or loss of loved ones. My mother fears running out of gas on the highway. She is a woman obsessed. As soon as the tank gets down to 3/4 full, she is convinced that if she doesn't get to a gas station *immediately*, she is going to be stranded on an empty stretch of road and left either to die of thirst or be massacred by a gang of Hell's Angels.

My father, on the other hand, loves to see just how many miles he can eke out of one tank. I have seen him coast to gas stations. I have seen him drive on fumes.

So all of our family vacations are interchangeable in my mind; the only thing I remember clearly are two adults screaming at each other from Maine to Florida about gasoline.

—Dave M., 23, graduate student, Washington, D.C.

✳   ✳   ✳   ✳

Every summer Mom and Dad packed up all of us kids in the minibus and we'd head out to some national park and pretend to have a good time. The problem was that food was central to my mother's life—health food, specifically. She was a fanatic. She was always packing up massive amounts of healthy food and insisting we eat it, even though the primary reason Dad accompanied us on these trips was so that he could eat crap he wasn't allowed to eat at home. Every recipe she made called for things like raw milk, goat cheese, and fresh butter without salt. Assembling the ingredients for her recipes would take ten times longer than making the food. Most days would end with Mom huddled over the portable hot plate she brought with us, whipping up some tofu patties, and Dad sneaking out to the Sizzler for a juicy steak and fries none of us kids was allowed to have.

—Francine N., 34, photographer, Houston, Texas

*   *   *   *

I have about forty rolls of film from my childhood I've titled Travels in the Ozone. Because every summer, for the first sixteen years of my life, this is what it was like: We would rent a car and set out with my father at the wheel. After God knows how much time—my parents believed no trip was a vacation unless it took at least ten hours to get there—we would approach our destination. After going around a few circles in the wrong direction, my mother would offer to drive. My father would have none of it. He would tell my mother he knew what he was doing and not to criticize. He would say all this while turning onto a street and pulling into a wrong lane. Then he would blame us for making him lose his concentration. We closed our eyes. My mother would say some prayers. Just as we were arriving at what I thought was picturesque scenery, I would get out my camera; my father would announce he knew where we were and keep driving. I pointed out some open parking spots for him, and his response was, "What, you want to stop? Just put your camera out the window, and I'll slow down a bit."

Every destination was the same. I have rolls upon rolls of film where, hey, that blur could be a sheep, or then again it could be a cathedral.

—Cindy M., 29, stylist, Miami, Florida

*   *   *   *

In 1963, we sailed—in steerage—from New York to Genoa on the S.S. *DaVinci*. The ship galloped in the waves. My parents didn't believe in Dramamine, and we were four little fat boys from Utah who'd never sampled the delights of cheap Italian cooking.

So there we were, one day out of New York, in the tail end of a hurricane. The doors swung open on this landing. The full rich aroma of Southern Italian cooking came wafting out, and I lost it right there in front of the doors of the dining room.

The next year, we did the exact same trip, only the weather was much, much worse. Did my parents learn anything from the year before? Not a chance. The five of us puked our way across the Atlantic. "Don't worry," they told us. "You'll get your sea legs."

—Dennis D., 42, football coach, Boston, Massachusetts

* * * *

My father fancied himself a mechanic, despite the fact that what he knew about cars could fit into . . . well, into a Yugo. I was thirteen when my father decided it was time for the two of us to hit the road; I think he had some sort of weird father-son-Kerouac bonding thing going on in his head. For some reason this little road trip of ours necessitated days of tinkering with his Camaro. This car was the Sunny von Bulow of motor vehicles: By all rights it should have given up the ghost ten years ago. At some point he decided that he needed someone to press on the gas to test his handiwork, so he said, "Son, get in there. . . ." Having grown up watching *Dukes of Hazzard*, I assumed there was only one way to press a gas pedal. I floored it. This gas-guzzling hulk of metal let out a roar, and smoke shot out from under the hood almost as fast as my father did.

After Dad got back from the emergency room, our trip was put off awhile. Like, twenty years.

—Arnold P., 28, sales rep, Baltimore, Maryland

* * * *

A Chip off the Old Block
(or, "What Do You Mean You Can't Be Just Like Us?")

Canny parents begin their brainwashing early. You say you're good in English? What d'ya think, you'll be the next Hemingway? So—your performance as Eliza Doolittle in My Fair Lady *won the school prize? Acting?! It's your choice, of course. If you want to spend the rest of your life waiting tables, be my guest.*

Whatever subject in school you enjoy, whatever seems to come most naturally to you—that's the career to avoid, because doing what comes naturally is just too easy. And you're not the type to take the easy way out, are you?

The career of choice in my family was, of course, medicine. Never mind that the mere mention of certain words (epiglottis, phlegm) was enough to send me gagging out of the room or that the sum total of my knowledge of organic chemistry was that, if I were in a bad mood, I could create a nice toxic cloud over the tristate area with a few vats of picric acid and sodium hydroxide. No. Whatever happened,

I would attend medical school. Oh, sure, if I were a real wuss, I could always become a psychologist. Of if I insisted on being a wacky free spirit, there was always law school. But writing? Unless I planned to become Judith Krantz or Danielle Steel, writing was a career track that inevitably led straight to alcoholism and a really tacky wardrobe. Time to wake up and smell the formaldehyde.

Twelve years after I graduated college, my mother still renews my annual subscription to the New England Journal of Medicine, *in hopes that one day I'll see the light. No amount of success in my chosen career can convince her I won't someday be tidying up rooms at a Motel 6.*

* * * *

The first argument I clearly remember between my mother and father happened when I was five: I had brought home a picture of a large spherical object dotted with purple spots, which in my mind was a perfect rendition of a cow. Within minutes I could hear them furiously fighting in stage whispers in the other room: "Frances, we've *got* to tell her," my father hissed. "She's *never* going to make it as an artist."

—Joan N., 32, journalist, New York, New York

* * * *

My dad was determined to raise his children to be self-sufficient. So in our house, it was not enough for my father to fix something, no; no matter how small the repair, it had to assume the proportions of a Westinghouse Science Project before he was satisfied.

For example, our house is on the bottom of a hill, and we've been flooded three times. First, through the basement drain: Dad fixed that one with one of those floating-ball thingies that allow water down, but not up, the drain. Next, water came up through the standpipe of the washer. Dad made a cap that screws on tight, which we would put on during storms. Finally, water came through the toilet on the first floor. At that point, Dad (and his three slave-labor sons) installed drain tile all the way around the basement and put a check valve in the sewer.

Quite a bit of effort—but was this enough for my father? No, sirree. The water became the central preoccupation of his life. Inside the check valve, Dad made a small electro-mechanical switch that would turn a light on whenever the check valve was shut—for no other reason than he *could*. Once he got the sump pump working, Dad measured the volume of water each cycle spewed out and how long the average cycle lasted. Then he hooked up an analog clock that turned on only when the pump ran, so he could tell how much water was cycled out of the sump. He then made charts of this, along with daily (or was it weekly?) rainfall, so he could see how well his contraption was working. I remember for weeks—for *months*—these charts were our main conversation over dinner, until it got to the point where the three of us agreed to get up and leave the table if he dared utter the word *water*.

At the first sign of trouble in my own house, I call the plumber.

—Randy C., 39, accountant, Rockport, Maine

* * * *

I'm so proud of my mother now, but when I was growing up I desperately wanted her to be like the other suburban mothers—you know, a pie-baking, Girl Scout–leading, PTA kind of mom. She just wasn't capable of it. My mother was a radiologist, and, much to my horror, every year she would volunteer for Parents Career Day at school. It wasn't enough for her to come in and tell us about being a doctor, oh, no; my mother had to have a whole dog-and-pony show. She'd come in, dressed in her lab coat (my mother's about 5'3'' and pretty much spherical), and she'd do a little dance with this real human skeleton she called Mr. Bones. Then she'd bring in a supply of chocolate barium, so all the kids could have a cup while they listened to a lecture she called Fun with Your Intestines. Actually, the other kids thought it was great, but I always wanted to melt into the floor.

Of course, now I see things a little differently. I can't wait to go into my daughter's second-grade class and give a little lecture about oral hygiene.

—Susan B., 36, dentist, Denver, Colorado

✳   ✳   ✳   ✳

My dad was a local fireman in a small California town, and he was convinced there was no better job on earth. His major preoccupation in life was infusing me with this same ambition, despite the fact that fire fighting was about as interesting to me as watching paint dry.

My father was very active in this group that was lobbying the city council to expand the fire department. With typical bureaucratic logic, the council decided to buy a five-story hook and ladder engine, despite the fact that the tallest building in this town was only three stories. The council's response? Some day the extra height will come in handy.

So there's my dad and the other guys sitting in the firehouse one day soon after the new truck's come in, just itching to use it. A call comes in from an old lady who says her cat's stuck in a tree. Needless to say, the fire department decides that the new hook and ladder should go out and prove all the critics wrong. Once they arrived—Dad at the wheel—it took only moments to rescue the poor cat. Pleased with their success and happy about being able to use the new engine, the truck loaded up, revved up, and drove off— right over the cat.

The lady sued the city for killing her cat. And years later, this town still doesn't have a building over three stories.

—Clarence J., 27, hairstylist, Los Angeles, California

✳   ✳   ✳   ✳

Looking back, this was one of the best things that ever happened to me. At the time, though, you would have been hard-pressed to convince me it was for my own good.

I have the utmost respect for my father: He's a motivated go-getter who started working for financial independence at the age of thirteen. Years later, his hard work meant he could provide his family with a quality of life he didn't have when *he* grew up. So naturally, the three of us were brats, with little understanding of the value of money or hard work.

Anyway, I was about twelve, spending another lazy summer doing as little as possible as often as possible. One weekend morning, my father woke me and asked me to do the lawn. I bitched and moaned and told him that if he was going to make me do work around the house, he'd have to pay me. He thought about it for a second and said he'd give me five bucks.

A few hours later, the lawn was done. He asked me to skim the pool and straighten up the pool area. I asked for five more bucks—making my case that this wasn't part of the original lawn-mowing deal. He obliged, and I spent an hour cleaning the pool.

When he asked me to help him clean out the garage, I asked for another five and got it without argument.

That evening, I sat in my bedroom and played with my money. My father walked in and asked where I would be staying that evening. "Here" was my obvious response.

"That'll be fifteen dollars," he said.

—Jack L., 28, airplane mechanic, Baltimore, Maryland

✳ ✳ ✳ ✳

In second grade I was really into science and inventors. My father knew this, and he was always on the lookout for father-and-son things to do. This could be pretty scary, as he was not the most technologically sophisticated person on the planet.

One day he decided that he would give me a lesson in how Thomas Edison invented the lightbulb. He got a vitamin bottle and a single strand of magnet wire that he had stripped off some household appliance. He then proceeded to plug the bare wires into the wall outlet. Even as a second grader, I knew this wasn't such a good idea, since Edison had had some trouble with air, but no one knew about wire resistance at the time.

That was the last father-and-son thing we did for a while—until Dad got out of the hospital.

—Jack L., 17, high-school student, Hope, Missouri

✳   ✳   ✳   ✳

God, I loved my first reporting job. I was twenty-two, and I had seen one too many B movies about hard-bitten, hard-nosed reporters. I was on the police beat, and I wouldn't let anyone forget it. I think I was smoking cigarillos.

In any case, at this time I was living at home, on the second floor of a three-family house, with my mom living on the first floor. We were in a small, idyllic New England town, the kind where a stolen bicycle was front-page news. Still, I had lots of late-night meetings—God knows why, as nothing of any consequence ever happened—and one night I got home around 2 A.M. Next morning, when I checked into work, I stopped at the police station—part of my usual routine, just in case that serial axe-murder story I was waiting to report on broke in the middle of the night. When I got there, everyone was kind of grinning. It seems my mother, worried that I hadn't come home, had not only called my editor, but also the police station, looking for me.

So much for being one of the boys.

—Carmen G., 35, newspaper reporter, New Hope, Pennsylvania

✳   ✳   ✳   ✳

My father is a well-known director of television shows and commericals, and when I was little he'd bring me on lots of shoots with him. All my friends thought this was the coolest thing—the glamour of hanging around with actors and models, shooting in all these beautiful spots, etc., etc. I was bored out of my skull. I could never understand what the hell was so exciting about sitting out in the hot sun doing the same thing over and over with a bunch of egomaniacal dickbrains. As a result, my father was always hiring my friends as interns. He couldn't believe everyone but his own kid thought his life was perfect.

With my dad's help, a lot of my friends have gone into careers in film and television. But if you ask me, I'm the lucky one. They're spending all their money on shrinks and divorces, and, as their accountant, I get to save their asses.

—Max D., 36, accountant, Beverly Hills, California

* * * *

I didn't know what my dad did for a living; in England, among the people I knew, one didn't talk about such things. I just know that there were certain times when my father was in his drawing room and he wasn't to be disturbed.

One day, I did the unthinkable: I burst into the drawing room without knocking. There was my father, bent over his desk, picking through a pile of diamonds with a pair of tweezers. I stood there for a second; he saw me and started yelling at the top of his voice. I panicked and ran away, terrified.

For weeks thereafter, I was caught in the most horrible dilemma: Should I go to the police? My father, I had decided, was a diamond thief. I was only about seven or eight; I figured the only reason he had yelled at me was because I had caught him sifting through his booty.

Finally, after literally weeks of keeping this secret to myself, I divulged everything to my mother: I decided she would know best whether or not to turn my father in.

She explained to me that he was, in fact, a diamond merchant, and he was allowed to have diamonds at home. He had yelled because he didn't want me to tell any of my little friends, since there's always a certain danger in keeping so many valuables on the premises.

Well, I cannot tell you the *relief* . . . anyway, I remember this as the moment when I realized I, too, wanted to go into the business. Even now, the idea of dealing with diamonds gives me a feeling of almost illicit excitement.

—Lawrence D., diamond merchant, London, England

* * * *

The first thing you have to realize is that when my brother and I were growing up, we lived a *long* way from civilization (or at least the nearest town). We grew up near the Grand Canyon. My father had a couple of small mining claims and also did some ranching on the old homestead. During most of the year, we lived in town so we could go to school, and my father worked for the Park Service.

About four to eight weeks of every summer, we would move out to the property to do whatever needed to be done to keep the fences up, etc. One thing about building earth dams and digging fence-post holes in hard rock: The only way to do it is to blast. When I was about twelve, and my brother about nine, my father was showing us how to set the black-powder wedges to blow postholes out, and by the next year we had graduated to setting caps and dynamite to blow the rock out of dams. Within another year or so, we were setting off whole boxes of dynamite, one hundred-pound kegs of Prell—the stuff they used at the World Trade Center bombing—and C3. (You have to realize that the United States was still civilized at that time, so it was easy for anyone to get these things.)

Naturally, not being satisfied with setting off a few explosions each summer, we managed to get one of the local mines to sell us leftover dynamite, which we would then go out in the boondocks and blow things up with. We got good at figuring out the right combination of delay caps, primacord, Prell, and whatever else was available to make some pretty spectacular explosions.

It all came to an end when I was about sixteen, when my father got another job and we moved away. At that point we were reduced to blowing up sand hills, which is not too much fun. Eventually my brother and I both ended up joining the Navy so we could graduate to blowing up some *really* good stuff. . . .

—Jim W., 32, captain, U.S. Navy, San Antonio, Texas

*   *   *   *

"So Why Aren't You Married Yet?"

My mother's desperation to see me married was equalled only by the worthlessness of her attempts to achieve her end. These days, she subscribes to what I call the Bookend Theory of Sexual Compatibility: She matches people by height. Whenever I tell her about a friend's new romance, her first question is not "What's he like?" or even "What does he do?"; it's "How tall is he?" As long as they look right together, my mother reasons, they'll be right. I'm about 5'10", and, thanks to my mother, I have had dates with an unusually large number of tall men with whom I had nothing in common. This has not stopped her from commenting—after I've complained about yet another date with a man who spent three hours telling me about his collection of photos of Saturn— "Yes, but he was tall, wasn't he?"

✳ ✳ ✳ ✳

I'm thirty-seven; every month now, for the last few years, I've been receiving a package of newspaper clippings from my mother. They contain bridal photos of singularly unattractive women; under each one, my mother writes in bold capitals: **IF THIS WOMAN CAN FIND A HUSBAND, WHY CAN'T YOU?**

—Sandy O., 38, travel agent, Portland, Oregon

✳   ✳   ✳   ✳

I was twenty-five and making my big move away from home—from Massachusetts to Connecticut. I was so pleased with myself and my newfound independence. But that didn't prevent one insidious thought from creeping into my head: *This trip will be fun! I'll take my mother!* A few days after I asked her to come see my new apartment with me, she called me up and said, "Guess what? You're father's going to come, too!" Which immediately transformed this trip into "Little Debbie and Her Parents Go to the Big City."

So there I was, with my first official teaching job and my first official apartment all to myself, both parents in tow. At the rental office, there was another person signing a lease, a gentleman about my age. I stared hard at my mother, desperately trying to telegraph the message, *No! Don't do it! Don't ask him!*

Of course, the message went unheeded. As I stood there like a ventriloquist's dummy, my mother's voice took on that oily quality I knew so well as she purred to the stranger, "So, are you single?" He was, and so were the next two men who came into the office.

Like one of those plate jugglers on the old *Ed Sullivan Show,* trying to keep several plates in the air simultaneously, my mother leapt from one conversation to the other; all the time, I could practically see the silent cartoon balloon over her head: *Which one of these is the right one for my daughter?* I was sure they could see it, too. When she decided on the one she liked best (the one who, interestingly, resembled my father), she simply told him which apartment I was moving into—and told him if he needed any more information, he should call her. She gave him her home number.

For about a month I didn't set foot outside my apartment until I made sure the coast was clear.

—Debbie M., 27, social studies teacher, Middletown, Connecticut

✳   ✳   ✳   ✳

How's this for a subtle double message? My father always claimed he couldn't wait for me to meet the man I was going to marry; whoever that was, he assured me, he knew he would regard this man as a son, because Dad had the utmost faith in my judgment.

Yet whenever I actually *did* work up the courage to invite someone over to meet him, after the preliminaries (job, hobbies, etc., etc.) Dad would somehow work the conversation around to a discussion of his penile implant. After my mother died, my Dad . . . well, let's just say my parents had married young, he hadn't had much of a social life, he had had diabetes, which affected his potency a bit, and he was determined to make up for lost time. So whenever I brought anyone over, if I left the room for *even a second,* I would come back to my boyfriend, pale and sweaty, and my dad saying something like, "Yup, with this prosthesis I'm ready whenever, wherever, whoever. . . ."

Think there may have been just the teeniest, tiniest male competition thing going on there?

—Lynn S., sociology professor, Austin, Texas

* * * *

When I turned thirty-one, a little bell went off in my mother's head that told her I was long overdue for marriage. Suddenly every girl she met was beautiful, well bred, had a good job, etc. Finally she fixated on this one girl, who, she informed me, was "as beautiful as a model, smart, and has a great sense of humor." Hmmm. Sounded good to me.

I lived in another state, and I planned to visit home at Christmas. When my mother casually informed me she was having a Christmas party and asked would it be okay to bring this girl along, I thought, *Well, why not?*

What she didn't mention was that this Christmas party would be a sit-down dinner: my mother, my aunt, my grandmother, my grandmother's best friend, and me. *And* the girl. Essentially, I had to meet this girl under the scrutinizing eyes of a gang of seventy-year-olds who'd make the Supreme Court look like the roadies on a Lollapalooza tour.

The girl and I met. She was very pretty and sweet, but I'm into vivacious, somewhat insane women, and this one was a pharmacist. Get the picture? After about ten minutes of conversation, I was aware of the clock in the kitchen ticking. I could hear plaster cracking off the walls upstairs. My mother was flitting around acting like this was the Christmas party she'd been dreaming about for months. In desperation I told a few jokes. I'm a policy wonk in my off-hours, so I reeled off a couple of sanitized surefire Clinton jokes.

Silence. The oldsters didn't get it, and neither did my "date." My heart started beating fast. I wanted to scream, *"Help me, I'm being sucked into a bottomless blind date Vortex of Hell."*

Instead, I kept smiling, which was just as well, since the scariest part was yet to come. Anyone who wasn't lobotomized could see the girl and I had nothing to say to each other, but that didn't prevent my mother and grandmother from trying everything in their power to keep that girl in her seat. Every time she tried making polite noises—"Oooh! It's getting late!"—my mother would lunge at her with another cup of coffee or a plate of cookies. "Stay! Stay awhile longer," Mom exhorted every time the girl stood up. Suddenly this girl and I had something in common: We *both* wanted to flee.

Finally I struck a bargain with my mother. She would let the poor girl leave after I finished a cup of hot tea. I very nearly threw the tea into my face. With scalding water streaming from my mouth I stood and grabbed the girl by the arm. We almost ran to the front door, my mother and grandmother in hot pursuit.

"Nearly home safe," I thought, but I was wrong. I opened the door and the girl scooted out. I stood on the threshold and waved good night. My mother and grandmother stood behind me. Suddenly I felt a steely hand in the middle of my back. With a strength that would do any twenty-year-old sailor proud, my grandmother shoved me out the door, and I stumbled into the street. I heard a slam, and the door shut behind me.

In the dark I tried to regain my composure. The girl stood staring at me. "Uh, well, g'night," I offered lamely. She looked so horrified at the prospect that I might touch her that she backed down our front steps, not noticing a little garden gnome my mother had placed strategically at the bottom of the staircase. She . . . well, she sort of catapulted down the steps, one leg acting as a kind of guillotine. She decapitated our gnome.

This was the last time I let my mother fix me up with anyone—although it's three years later, and she's still trying.

—Jeff P., 34, sales rep, Decatur, Georgia

✳   ✳   ✳   ✳

About every six months, since I turned thirty, my mother has insisted on taking a roll of photos of me, so she can show them to friends of hers who have sons. So every six months we have the same fight: I tell her I'll pose for the pictures if she gives me final say about which pictures she shows. She always assures me I'll be consulted. Then, when the pictures are developed, she refuses to show them to me, claiming that only a mother can tell when her child is shown off to best advantage. I have a feeling she purposely picks photos that make me look like a Stepford wife.

—Lana, 38, art director, Napa, California

✳   ✳   ✳   ✳

Mom has a fifties/Tupperware kinda view of the world. On the one hand, she respects and admires my feminist ideals; on the other, she thinks I'm doomed to eternal unhappiness. Every time I phone a young man instead of waiting for him to call me, she puts her head in her hands and sighs, "There goes another one."

My father wants me to go to graduate school so I can

meet someone nice. He doesn't particularly care what I go back to school for; for some reason, his theory is, All the Good Ones Are Still in School. Apparently he hasn't hung around with too many male graduate students. Every grad student I've ever met (law and med students excepted) has been totally infantilized by the process—a whole generation of twenty-five-year-olds who have no problems being parasites. Just what I need—a man to baby-sit. As if I weren't already a full-time baby-sitter for myself.

—Maryanne C., 24, news reporter, St. Louis, Missouri

✳   ✳   ✳   ✳

My father loves me, but I was never his idea of a great beauty: In other words, I did not have anorexia, bleached-blond hair, and surgically enlarged boobs like his first three wives. When I turned twenty-five and was somewhat low on marriage prospects, he decided to take things into his own hands. Dad owned a thriving auto-supply business; he put a picture of me up on the bulletin board at work, with a notice saying that *any guy who wanted to take me out would be paid overtime for the number of hours we were out on a date.*

At first I didn't know about the ad; I was surprised when I started getting calls from guys who worked for my father. And then I found out. Amazing, isn't it, that I waited until I was thirty to go into therapy. . . .

To this day, no one can explain to my father why there was anything wrong with his approach. You ask him about this incident even now, and he'll shrug and say, "Hey, it was worth a shot."

P.S. I've married a great guy who thinks I'm the most

gorgeous creature on earth. Everyone says he looks like my father.

—Cindy A., 23, secretary, Wilmington, Pennsylvania

* * * *

My mother and my grandmother were forever conspiring to marry me off, although it was pretty obvious to anyone with a set of eyes that I was a lesbian. I went to visit Nana in Florida over spring break, and she set me up on *three* blind dates (all of which I refused). Finally she resorted to ambushing me with men at her club swimming pool: "This is Mark. He's prelaw at Rutgers. . . ."

When I finally came out to my dad, he was none too pleased. Still, he appreciated my taste in menswear. He would always take me shopping, and we would shop for ties for both of us. Although he recognized I had a better sense of style than anyone else in our family, he'd grumble the whole time, "Why won't you wear feminine clothes?"

I would tell him, "I am female, therefore anything I wear is feminine." Oy.

Then there was the time I came home excitedly and told my mother I had just purchased my first pair of spikes. She was so happy, which I thought was rather strange. When I took them out of the box, her face dropped. They were cleated softball shoes; she thought I'd bought spike heels.

—Nina T., nightclub owner, New York, New York

* * * *

I'm from Virginia, and I was leaving to take a great new job in Nebraska. This was a very important position for me at a noted zoological research institute there. Other mothers might wish their daughters luck, or Godspeed, or break a leg, or whatever. My mother? As I was getting ready to board the plane, she flung her arms around me and started to sob: *"Please get married before I die."*

—Gabrielle S., 27, zoologist, Omaha, Nebraska

* * * *

My mom suffers from what I call "You Just Never Know" syndrome. She's talked me into going out on dates with petty drug dealers, spiritual healers, Quasimodo—you name it.

I still remember Rudy Mirales and my senior prom. Rudy was this beer-guzzling dude from the kind of New Jersey high school where the prom is the highlight of every girl's life, and afterward everyone gets a job at Stuckey's.

Anyway, Rudy asked me out, and I told him I'd be out of town for the prom. My mom overheard this conversation on the phone and was furious—she made me call him back and say I'd *love* to go to the prom with him.

He was drunk when he picked me up and proceeded to get drunker. Suffice it to say that I ended the evening in my pink frou frou dress at the local make-out point, screaming, *"Take me home,"* to a man vomiting over the edge of a cliff.

—Amanda C., 24, department-store fashion buyer,
  Orange, New Jersey

* * * *

I don't mind that my mother tries to set me up with people—except for this one habit she has: Invariably, she leaves out some obvious, important detail about this person and claims later she "forgot." Last week she fixed me up with a man with a hook arm.

Now, there's nothing *wrong* with a hook arm, but it's just the kind of thing a girl should know about beforehand, you know? I just said "beforehand" didn't I? Well, that's what I did all evening. I couldn't bring myself to ask him how he'd lost his arm, but I'd manage to say things to him like, "Are you as hooked on movies as my mother tells me?"—and then I'd want to *die*.

—Amy A., 25, flight attendant, Newark, New Jersey

✳   ✳   ✳   ✳

My mother just retired as an English professor at Columbia University, and every time my sister and I start dating someone new, we are subject to what we call the Catechism:

Where did he go to college?
What did he major in?
What was his grade point average?
Where did he go to high school?
What other colleges did he apply to?
What were his SAT scores?

We are expected to uncover this information on our first date. This might not have seemed unreasonable ten years ago, but time marches on. Not that many men in their thirties remember what they got on their SATs—and if they do, perhaps that fact alone should set off a few alarm bells.

—Karen D., 35, political fund-raiser, Washington, D.C.

✳   ✳   ✳   ✳

❚ didn't come out to my parents so much as they discovered my sexuality and I confirmed it, but one thing I noticed was that they never used the words *gay, homosexual,* or even any of the lesser-liked versions of same. They always talked about me being "That Way." Occasionally, I would hear my mother talking to a friend on the phone, one with a daughter—my mother seemed to know an inordinate number of women with daughters who needed to be fixed up—and I'd hear her sigh and say, "Sorry, what can we do? He's 'that way.' "

For years I wondered what "That Way" was. Was I brought to them by a UFO? Did I mutter obscenities at strangers? Did I projectile-vomit in church?

My parents have finally accepted my lifestyle, but to this day I've never heard them use the word *gay.* I guess they want it "that way."

—Jeremy S., 34, hairdresser, Tulsa, Oklahoma

✳   ✳   ✳   ✳

❚ wish you could hear this telephone answering-machine tape I have of my mother—I kept it for several years. She had fixed me up with this cute blond boy, the son of some people she had gone to college with. That's what finding a mate for her daughter was all about: finding in-laws she wanted to be friends with.

So at any rate, I went out with this guy; he was a psychiatrist teaching at Harvard, and therefore only marginally sane. He sang in a choral group, a fact I filed under "Diverse Interests." But there was simply no chemistry whatsoever. Have you ever met a man who you know immediately is the one who gets drunk on two glasses of wine at the party and then wants everyone to join him in a chorus of "Copacabana?" This was *that* guy. I admitted to my mom I didn't expect to see him again.

Immediately she jumped to the conclusion that I had done something to botch this golden opportunity. She left me *five* consecutive messages, saying things like, "Lori, please, just give him a call. You just have to compliment him . . . just say you like his tie." Each time she called, she gave me a different idea of what I should do. *"Please, please, just do me this one favor. . . ."* It didn't occur to her for a second that *I* didn't care for him. After all, I was thirty-eight; my ovaries were about to give up the ghost.

Finally, to please her, I went out on one more date. Pleased with his conquest, Dr. Demento spent most of the evening explaining his theory of the widening chasm between the sexes, why men can't commit, why *he* can't commit (although maybe I'd be The Lucky Woman to Change All That), and how we should proceed very, very slowly just to see how things go. Then he allowed me to pick up the check.

—Lori S., 40, photographer, Menlo Park, California

✳   ✳   ✳   ✳

Introducing a Significant Other to Your Parents
"Mom, Dad, Meet the Person You're Going to Torment for the Rest of Your Lives"

He is the most scintillating, adorable creature you've ever laid eyes on. Everything about him thrills you. Why is it, then, when he meets your parents, the man you perceive as Mel Gibson suddenly mutates into Yasir Arafat? It's the Parental Whammy: The tiniest chink in your beloved's armor becomes a gaping, raw wound.

You say she has the perfect body for those clingy dresses she favors? Forget her Phi Beta Kappa key: Your parents think she bumps and grinds for dollars at Show World. So Mr. Right is a world-class skier, an ace race-car driver, a man whose daredeviltry leaves you breathless? Oh, a perfect match, your parents say with a sigh—as long as you don't mind being a widow at forty.

How do you turn your beloved's personality quirk into a personality disorder? Introduce him/her to your parents.

* * * *

There's nothing that threatens a Jewish household more than the thought of people who are *better* Jews than they are. My parents are reformed Jews. Very reformed. The kind that has both a Hanukkah bush and a Christmas tree. Essentially, we celebrated anything that involved getting gifts. Anyway, my fiancé, who was orthodox, was coming to the house for the first time for Thanksgiving—what I thought of as a nice, *neutral* holiday. I explained to my parents that he had a wonderful sense of humor, but he took the kosher laws very seriously. So let's respect them, okay?

When Bert came to the door, my father was standing ready with a gleaming silver bowl. "Shrimp?" he asked politely.

Things went downhill from there. My mother had decided to prepare two *completely different* meals, including two turkeys—one kosher (no mixing of meat and milk products) and one non-kosher. So the entire dinner was filled with conversation like, "Would you pass the normal turkey, please?"

Eventually, as you may have guessed, the engagement broke up. Now I date only WASPs.

—Joan N., 32, journalist, New York, New York

*   *   *   *

My mother has an uncanny knack for deflating my most joyous moments. When I was about seventeen, I started going out with this very quiet, sweet guy. He was my first boyfriend and I was so excited—I had begun to believe I would die dateless.

One morning I was quietly eating breakfast with my mother, minding my own business, when she leaned over and, out of the clear blue sky, remarked, "Roger's a very nice boy, but he really doesn't have much personality, does he?"

I was crestfallen.

The worst thing was, she had a point.

—Patty P., 24, graduate student, Topeka, Kansas

* * * *

A few years back, when I was going through an awful divorce, I brought my new fiancée home to meet my parents. I had managed to put off this event for about a year, but the new woman in my life, Joanie, was determined to meet them. I explained that, simply put, my mother was demented; Joanie'd say, "Oh, I'm sure she's just idiosyncratic." I explained about my dad being an alcoholic, etc. Her response to that was: "Well, hey, whose dad isn't?"

We walked in the door, and my father had already passed out. The first thing my mother said to Joanie was, "Oh, you're my son's next willing victim!" Mom proceeded to spend the next four hours telling Joanie how successful and happy her life would have been if she'd never had children.

Later that day Joanie told me, "I'm sorry I doubted you. You were right. Your mom really *is* crazy."

It was a great adulthood moment.

—Fred T., 45, book publisher, New York, New York

* * * *

My new boyfriend Josh had joined us for dinner. I mistakenly told my father that, instead of compulsive eaters, we were *convulsive* eaters—at which point, he started to fake a seizure. Everyone thought this was a scream, of course, except me and Josh; I hadn't told them my boyfriend had epilepsy.

—Heather, 21, aerobics instructor, Midland, Texas

✳   ✳   ✳   ✳

My then-fiancée (now my wife), Laurie, wrote some mystery stories for a "fanzine" before I met her. Since my mother likes mysteries, I decided to bring a copy of the magazine back home from college before they met so they would have something to talk about. About three days later, my mother called. She questioned me closely about one of the stories Laurie had written that involved a woman who kills her husband and buries him under their new patio. But when Mom and Laurie met, everything was great. Five years later, the story was still in my mother's mind. At that point Laurie and I were building a new house, and we showed the blueprint to Mom. When I pointed out the patio, she paused for a moment and said, "That's nice . . . how are the two of you getting along?"

—Bert S., 40, lawyer, Lansing, Michigan

✳   ✳   ✳   ✳

My wife and I met while I was stationed in the Navy in Naples, Italy. When we decided to get married, she arranged a trip home to Tennessee to tell her parents. The conversation went something like this:

"Mom, Dad, I'm going to get married."

"Oh, no. He's not an Italian?"

"No, no. He's from New York City."

"Oh, my God. That's worse."

—Eric E., 52, insurance executive, Nashville, Tennessee

✳   ✳   ✳   ✳

In 1977, my boyfriend came to meet my parents for the first time. Keep in mind, I went to an all-girl Catholic school and he was from a local coed public school (something my parents were not too happy about in the first place).

He arrived carrying a bowling bag. My mother, being the gracious hostess she is, inquired about the bag. My boyfriend just smiled nervously and said nothing. She asked again, and he said, "Uh, just some, you know, stuff." You'd think he might have just said, "A bowling ball," but, let's face it, this guy wasn't too swift.

Sensing an interesting lie here, my mother waited until Jack went to the bathroom to run over and unzip the bag. The last thing I remember seeing was a white blur as my mother, in her nurse's uniform, streaked to the kitchen sink and threw up. Out of the bag slithered Yvette, a six-foot boa constrictor my boyfriend was "baby-sitting" for a friend.

—Erin T., 32, hardware store owner, Newark, New Jersey

✳   ✳   ✳   ✳

When I was about sixteen, I met this French boy at the beach. We chatted a bit, and then I gave him my phone number—forgetting, for the moment, that my father was in the habit of interrogating anyone who called the house.

Jean-Marc called, and my father intercepted the call. At

my father's warmest, he's still a rather chilly individual; that day he was a veritable iceberg. After exchanging stiff formalities, he asked Jean-Marc where he met me. This smart-ass French boy was not used to being interrogated. He said to my father: "Well, I met her at the bar where she dances, of course."

"Dances?"

"At the Golden Palace."

The Golden Palace was our local topless bar. Now you have to understand, my breasts are small now, but at the time, my chest was virtually concave.

This inescapable detail did not prevent my father from buying Jean-Marc's story; in fact, at that moment, it didn't occur to him for a moment that his daughter *wasn't* a stripper in her spare time. It took me and my mother hours to convince him nobody would hire me for this kind of work.

Looking back on it, my father seemed to take more than a passing interest in his daughters' breasts. When my sister was in high school, she was going steady with a very nice boy; in fact, I think he was a Mormon. On her seventeenth birthday, the boy gave her what we all considered the perfect gift: a white cashmere sweater.

Everyone, that is, except my father. He made her return it. His reason? The implication of giving a sweater, my father said, was that he had assessed the size of her breasts to get the right size. It was an affront that he had chosen something so personal.

Needless to say, Dad was very protective of our virginity—to no avail, in my case.

—Lisa A., 34, government administrator, McLean, Virginia

✳   ✳   ✳   ✳

The first thing out of my father's mouth when he met my future wife, Annie? "You know, no woman's good enough for my son."

Now, I think lots of parents might think this, but few of them actually say it. And don't think Annie ever forgot it.

—Marshall G., 35, management consultant, Philadelphia, Pennsylvania

✳   ✳   ✳   ✳

My father did not have a knack for the graceful conversation segue. I'd have some new boyfriend over to dinner, and there'd be a pause in the conversation—at which point my father would pipe up with something safe and noncontroversial, like, "So, what do you think of abortion?"

—Maryanne C., 27, news reporter, St. Louis, Missouri

✳   ✳   ✳   ✳

I grew up in a Cuban family in Miami, and my mother practices Santeria, a mixture of Catholicism and voodoo. For years I thought there was nothing unusual about a mother who was a witch, since many of the mothers in the neighborhood where I grew up were. But my mother was an especially well-known one, and she made a tidy living casting spells for her friends.

Before I introduced her to my husband-to-be, I worried a little bit about her reaction to his religion: He comes from a pretty observant Jewish family.

So we walked into the house, and my mother, ignoring me, threw her arms around Benjamin. "Thank God! A Jew!" she cried. Ben was a bit startled: He hadn't expected quite that warm a reception.

As it happened, she was in the middle of some minor intra-family war that required a particularly strong good-luck charm to counteract a spell one of her brothers had put on her. One of the strongest good luck charms, according to my mother, was a Star of David—*"Because those Jews, they are a lucky people."* (How she came to that conclusion, I'm not quite sure.) Anyway, the charm was particularly powerful if an honest-to-God Jew *bought* it.

Now, you wouldn't think Jews were too hard to come by in Miami, but my mother didn't know any—and here was one, right in her very own house! We weren't allowed to sit down to dinner until Ben had driven downtown and purchased a Star of David.

Two weeks later—and I'm not saying Ben had anything to do with it—my mother's brother had a mild heart attack.

I don't believe in any of this stuff. I swear. Although I *did* have her freeze one of the partners in my law firm who'd been getting on my nerves. (Want to get someone out of your life? Write their full name on a slip of paper, submerge it in water in a small container, and put it in the freezer.)

I didn't have to work with the guy for months.

—Nikki G., 33, lawyer, San Francisco, California

✳   ✳   ✳   ✳

Weddings

If it weren't for the presents, would any of us really go through with it?

* * * *

To say my mother was perturbed by my marriage is like saying the Serbs are perturbed by the Bosnians: Her fight against me and Bob was an all-out nuclear assault. The problem is that my mother is a strict Catholic, and I had the audacity to be marrying a divorced man. Not only divorced, but with *children!* And I had been *living with him* before marriage! And—this is the worst part—he had only been separated when we started seeing each other.

Among the things Mother did: called Bob's boss at work and told him one of his employees was an adulterer; wrote notes to each of his four children, asking them if they knew what their dad was up to; called Bob's ex-wife, invited her to lunch, and got her to spill her guts about every heinous act my future husband had ever committed. Then, banding together, the ex-wife and my mother told me that if I had the nerve to go through with this thing, they would storm the ceremony and tell all our guests about the kind of people we really were.

That year, I probably had the only wedding in St. Paul, Minnesota, with armed guards.

—Jane D., 25, lawyer, St. Louis, Missouri

* * * *

For my sister's wedding, my parents grew a cow. Her name was Frieda.

At the age of forty-four, my mother had decided to become a dairy farmer, so by the time my sister was getting married Mum had been farming for about ten years. But these were cows raised for milk. Anyway, Frieda was a gorgeous red heifer, and Mom timed it so that Frieda would be perfectly fatted up for the wedding. We all talked about how delicious Frieda would be, how we'd have the best feast in the county, etc., etc.

What nobody anticipated was that we'd all fall in love with Frieda. By the time the wedding rolled around, we simply could not butcher her.

When my sister married, the main course was chicken.

Seven years have passed. Since that time, unfortunately, my sister's gotten divorced—but Frieda lives to moo another day.

—Lotte G., 35, barrister, London, England

* * * *

This took place three years ago, at my elder sister's wedding. An old-family Louisiana girl marries an old-family Vicksburg, Mississippi man. Lots o' flowers, candles, the works.

One of my younger sisters attended with her husband, and the other with her fiancé. For lack of a date, I took one of my friends who is, like me, a gay man. He'd already met most of my family.

Immediately after the ceremony, the family was gathering in one of those old Vicksburg turn-of-the-century mansions for pictures and a reception. The biggest debate (which I overheard, between the bride and my mother): Were they expected to include Kevin's "friend" in the pictures of the family, along with the other siblings' spouses/fiancés?

Actually, Michael and I weren't even dating, much less "a couple," and neither of us has ever said a word to my family about being gay. (Apparently, we don't have to.) The concerns were, would Michael be offended at being excluded? Would other family members ask too many questions about who this strange young man in the pictures was? Would my eighty-five-year-old dowager empress grandmother have a coronary if Michael stood with us? You get the idea. Inconsequential as it was, at that moment it was drama worthy of a Tennessee Williams play.

Eventually, the compromise reached was that "legal" family members would be included but not fiancés or what they assumed were "significant others"; this being done primarily to avoid disturbing my grandmother, who everyone's always been afraid of.

At the end of the reception, when Michael and I were leaving to drive back to Louisiana, my grandmother called me aside. Uh-oh, I thought, here it comes: the Are-You-Headed-for-Heaven-or-Babylon lecture.

Instead, Grandmother asked me to come to lunch in town with her sometime—and to bring my "little friend" with me. "You make sure he treats you right, now," were her parting words.

Oh, the gymnastics parents go through to protect those who don't need it!

—Sam B., 29, college professor, New Orleans, Louisiana

✳   ✳   ✳   ✳

My parents had just bought a posh house in Bel Air, and Mother decided my wedding was the ideal time to display her astounding hostessing talents and new money. So she invited about three hundred people, including, unbeknownst to me, the man she was having an affair with and *his entire family*. Then, inexplicably, she entrusted my fiancé with setting out the namecards for three hundred total strangers.

My mom was an hour late for the ceremony, making three hundred people wait and affording her the grand entrance she always wanted. Her reason? It was all the groom's fault. He hadn't grasped the social intricacies of seating arrangements for three hundred people he did not know—so she had to spend an hour rearranging them.

—Sarah C., 26, San Francisco, California

✳   ✳   ✳   ✳

I remember the days leading up to my marriage as a series of conversations escalating in mental damage.

The day I brought Karl to my house to announce our engagement, the first words out of my father's mouth were, "What do we really know about you? I've only met you a couple of times before in my life." My mother, determined to keep up her end of the conversation, followed my father's remark with, "Are those your real teeth?" What Mom was really trying to do was figure out whether Karl's perfect smile was the result of braces and whether, therefore, her future grandchildren would have wolf teeth that would eventually have to be rectified with thousands of dollars of orthodontic work. My mother, the geneticist.

We made it through that day. Sometime later, I was on my way to pick up my wedding license, when I made the mistake of stopping home to borrow my father's car. Then and there I was treated to a lecture about my future husband's perceived faults, from being an investment banker (and therefore slick, money-grubbing scum) to being short. The word *arrogant* came up a lot. He just couldn't imagine me making this kind of error in judgment. He had hardly met Karl, but that didn't stop him from launching a total character assassination.

Finally, my father came up for air. "So, what do you see in this man?" he asked pleasantly.

I didn't have time to answer before he informed me that he hoped I wasn't going to make the social gaffe of wearing white—because, since we had been living together, *that* was a total sham; and, by the way, he wouldn't walk me down the aisle to give me away. Obviously I had already given *myself* away.

—Patricia G., 31, elementary-school teacher, Hastings-on-Hudson, New York

* * * *

*This falls under the category of "Long-Lasting Scars Result-
ing from Letting Your Child Learn from Experience."*

I was about nine years old, and my parents and I were invited to a wedding of some member of our family. I was
something of a tomboy and also had a terrible complex
about money. (I was afraid that somehow my parents
wouldn't have enough, even though it was perfectly obvious
to anyone but a paranoid nine-year-old that we were com-
fortably middle class.)

My mom took me shopping for a dress for the wedding. I
tried on a beautiful lavender number with ruffles and frills,
which, deep down, I really liked. It cost thirty dollars. (This
was in 1971.) I also tried on a tennis dress—one of those
white sleeveless things with legs that are now called a "skort"
but then were "culottes." It cost ten dollars. My mother left
the decision to me. Being the thrifty kid I was, I thought,
"The tennis dress costs only ten dollars, and I'll get much
more use out of it than I will out of the other one."

I wore the tennis dress to the wedding. The feeling of being out of place, as if all eyes were upon me, was as horrifying as in one of those dreams where you show up to
school naked. I still dislike shopping and dressing for any
kind of formal event. And I always bring along someone
whose opinion I trust—*not*, needless to say, my mother.

—Audrey M., 25, tour guide, Rockport, Maine

✳   ✳   ✳   ✳

I had always yearned for the kind of mother who would be
keenly interested in my wedding day. I had images of the
two of us shopping for floral arrangements, getting my dress

fitted, ordering the cake. This mom of my dreams would make Florence Henderson look like Joan Crawford.

But when it came time to get married, my mother's major contribution to the event was showing up. That, and her one suggestion for the wedding procession: She felt that my husband and I should walk out together, next to last, and then *she* should be the final member of the party to emerge.

—Nikki G., 33, lawyer, San Francisco, California

✳ ✳ ✳ ✳

My mother, in all her hostessing wisdom, decided the best possible day for my wedding would be December 22. Finally, after years of attending her friends' children's weddings, she was going to show everybody how to throw a *real* party. No matter how many times I insisted that three days before Christmas was not the most convenient time for people, my mother insisted *she* knew what she was doing, and how could I dare question her—me, the woman who was known for throwing parties where everyone ran out of conversation in half an hour and ended up huddled around the TV set, playing *Jeopardy*? Thoroughly cowed, I then deferred to my mother in every wedding decision. (My fiancé, wisely, just stopped talking to everyone in my family.)

So the wedding was planned, and, ominously, the RSVPs were not pouring in. This did not disturb my mother, who insisted her friends were all "the spontaneous types." The hall was booked, the band hired, etc., etc. To make a long story short, out of 150 people invited about twenty showed up. Ten of them were one family with eight kids. My most vivid memory of my wedding day was watching my mother get stinking drunk, grab the microphone, and shriek, *"You can all go to hell! I've bought my last wedding present!"*

—Brenda G., 31, documentary producer, New York, New York

* * * *

Guilt: The Gift That Keeps on Giving

"Conscience," H. L. Mencken wrote, "is a mother-in-law whose visit never ends." Some of us not only let this mother-in-law stay—we give her our finest linens, our fluffiest pillows, and full access to our credit cards.

We are bound to our parents with velvet ropes. There is no bribe, no threat, no water torture that controls us as effectively as guilt. My mother (who lives about an hour's drive away) wants to go to lunch. I may have five deadlines, the onset of flu, and a dinner party I'm supposed to be giving that night. All I have to hear are those magic words: "That's okay. I'm sure there's someone else who'll enjoy spending time with me."

One hour later, you know where you'll find me.

* * * *

My mother uses presents as a weapon. You may not want any more strings attached than those already harpooned into your side, but no matter; she persists.

Here's the way it works: Mom wants to give me something; I say, "No." Then I say "No" until I'm hyperventilating with rage, and finally I say, "Yes." I give her some parameters about the gift in question—size, color, brand, whatever.

Then, several days later, she comes back to me with the grisly details of the purchase: The salesperson had to get it off the highest shelf in the store, it had to be specially ordered, she had to go to the tip of Long Island to get it, she had to go through one hundred boxes in the back room to find *exactly* what I wanted. One time she informed me the gift in question was such a hassle that she had to hire a delivery truck to get it home.

By the time I've received whatever it is, there's this mountain of obligation involved, since the gift represented a task of Herculean dedication that I, as the ungrateful daughter, could never hope to repay.

—May M., 25, congressional aide, Washington, D.C.

✳ ✳ ✳ ✳

I'm an only child, and there's nothing my father enjoys more than letting me know how much money he's saving on my behalf. Almost every day he'll call and say something like, "Honey, today I'm bringing to work a cheese sandwich I made myself; the sandwiches at the deli next door cost $4.50," or "Honey, today I cut my own hair."

My parents, incidentally, are easily worth a couple of million dollars.

—Moira S., 30, hospital administrator, New York, New York

* * * *

It's always been the family joke that you can't get my mother off the phone; she's a nonstop talker. And when I'm in some sort of rush, that's usually the time she calls me up and tries to engage me in a debate about the best kinds of cat food for my Persian, Winston.

This year she had a small stroke, which temporarily impaired her speech. She's fine now. But the first thing she did when I came to visit her in the hospital was slowly, shakily, write me this note: "Well, I guess you got your wish."

—Joan N., 32, journalist, New York, New York

* * * *

When I was very young, I used to put my shoes outside the bedroom door on December 6, so St. Nicholas could visit and put oranges and chocolate gold coins in them. I guess I had been particularly bad at that time, and I woke up to find coal in my shoes. I was devastated. I remember crying a lot. Not only because of the coal, but because I was afraid Santa wouldn't come. My parents sympathized and said that if I was on especially good behavior until Christmas I could redeem myself and Santa *would* come. Man, did I sweat out those few weeks.

Santa showed, by the way. I don't think they wanted to push their luck with coal in the stocking and nothing under the tree.

—Adam B., 24, farm manager, Fargo, North Dakota

* * * *

This was in the early eighties, when answering machines were still a novelty item. I had just gotten my first machine, so naturally I spent days trying to find the perfect obnoxious greeting, guaranteed to irritate anyone in under thirty seconds. One day, my mother was visiting, and I asked her if she wanted to leave the outgoing message—whatever she wanted to say.

So for about a year, this was what everyone heard when they rang my home: "This is Marcia's mother. Marcia is an only child; she never writes, she never calls. So why not give me a buzz? I'd be happy to talk to you. My number is XXX-XXXX."

Everyone called my mother. *Everyone*. She loved the attention.

—Marcia M., 27, actress, Fairfield, Connecticut

*   *   *   *

I was the only girl, with two slightly younger brothers. I always resented the fact that I had to do the dishes—the rest of the family would take off after dinner while I cleaned. But my mother had convinced me that I was the only one who could competently perform this service, and if the task was left to my brothers, we would all get ptomaine poisoning *and it would be my fault.*

One day I rebelled. Big scene, Mom angry, Dad scarce, boys grinning behind their hands. Mom screams, *"Okay, I'll make the boys do the dishes, but if they don't do a good job, you're going to have to do them again."*

You can pretty much imagine what happened from there. After a week of my brothers doing the work, nobody could find any pots or pans, because my brothers had hidden them under their beds. Since I didn't plan to spend the rest of my life as the dish police, I was soon back to doing the dishes. My mama didn't raise no fools.

—Paulina T., 23, nurse, Oxford, Mississippi

* * * *

When I was six, I broke my father's favorite pencil. I don't know how anyone *has* a favorite pencil, but my father did. It looked like every other No. 2 pencil you've ever seen since the beginning of time. But for a half hour—a very long time in the life of a six-year-old—my father gave me a lecture about how I never took care of anything I was given, how pencils cost money, how they don't just grow on trees. (I wish I had had the wherewithal to tell him that, in a sense, pencils *do* grow on trees. But, hey, I was six.)

As I got older, Dad upped the ante. When I was ten and crying my head off about how I didn't want to go to sleep-away camp (the counselor's main function at camp, I think, was to make sure you didn't leave), he showed me the bill for my eight-week stay. When I was eighteen and in my first semester at Amherst, he Xeroxed every bill the school sent him and mailed it to me.

To this day, I'm so obsessed with taking care of the things I have that I have agonizing pain if I so much as get a stain on my pants. Yesterday I bought a new pair of pants for twenty-two dollars, and I'm already depressed at the prospect that someday these pants will rip.

—Andrew M., 35, screenwriter, Putney, Vermont

* * * *

I was in eleventh grade, and my sister, Kathy, was in ninth grade. I couldn't get a girl to let me spend money on her, never mind feel her breasts—while meanwhile, my little sister was giving it away to anyone who owned a Camaro. Anyway, this is how I usually spent my Saturday night: I'd get stinking drunk with my pals, and I'd roll home about 1 A.M., at which point my mother would be sitting in the living room, weeping, "We don't know where your sister is! If you don't care about her honor, who will?" Her *honor?* I was just jealous that she was getting laid and I wasn't.

Then I'd be pushed out the door and told not to come back until I found her. I'd weave around on the roads until I found her, generally pulled over at some truck stop with a guy named Bubba. I'd go home and tell my mother she was "with friends." But if, God forbid, I didn't find her, *I'd* be the one to get in trouble.

—Nathan D., 20, auto mechanic, Athens, Georgia

* * * *

When I was growing up with my grandmother—she lived with us—we kept a kosher home. Whenever I asked my mother why we were kosher, my mother would reply, "It's for your grandmother. She wouldn't be comfortable if we weren't kosher."

Years went by, and always I got the same answer. One day, when I was a teenager and pretty damn fed up with the kosher routine, I turned to my mother and said, "Tell me once more—*why* do we have to keep kosher?"

My mother began her same tired explanation—"It's for your grandmother"—just at the moment my grandmother walked in the room. "You're keeping kosher for *me?*

Really? That's funny, because I couldn't care less. I thought we were keeping kosher for *you*."

Apparently Grandma had been keeping a stash of pork rinds under her bed or something.

That was the last day any of us kept kosher.

—Miriam G., 36, secretary, Miami, Florida

✳   ✳   ✳   ✳

Here's how gift-giving works in my family. Let's say it's Christmas.

Step 1. I tell my parents, "Give me a hint. What would you like for Christmas?"

Step 2. The parents register their protest:

Mom: "What do we need from our only daughter?"

Dad: "If you buy me anything, I'll return it."

Mom: "Come visit us—that's our gift."

Step 3. I ask them what they want about forty-seven times, and they refuse to tell me. I end up buying them presents specifically manufactured for gift-phobes like me—gifts that say, *"Nobody in their right mind would want this, but look how much money it costs."* A telephone shaped like a duck—that sort of thing. I then shut my mouth about gifts.

Step 4. Five days before Christmas, they start making noises about gifts—gifts their friends' children had given *their* parents. "You wouldn't believe it, that Baccarat crystal chandelier Sandra's daughter gave her. Who knew that girl was doing so well? She was never the brightest student . . . and yet, look, our daughter at the top of her class, and Sandra's daughter makes all the money! . . ."

Step 5. Christmas Eve. Certain I've bombed again, I rush out and buy several increasingly useless and pricey items, plus fifth-row center seats to *Cats*.

Step 6. The presents are opened; my parents ooh and ahh over everything. Then there's the pause. The pause before my father starts in on me: "You know, you just throw your money around like an idiot." At this point, my mother asks for all my receipts. ("This is exactly what I wanted, but it may not be *quite* the right size, darling. . . .")

Step 6. Several days after Christmas. Everything is returned (they send me back a check telling me to "put it toward our birthday gifts")—everything, that is, except the tickets to *Cats*. "Well," my mother says with a sigh, "we've seen it before, but if it means spending time with you, we'd *love* to see it again."

With a few minor variations, this has been going on for about ten years. But the truth is, it makes them happy. They get me to spend a lot of money on them, they get to disapprove of my spending habits, and they get to make me feel hopelessly inadequate—all in one fell swoop.

—Daria S., advertising copywriter, Boston, Massachusetts

* * * *

"Privacy? What Could You *Possibly* Have to Hide from the People Who Toilet Trained You?"

The KGB could have learned a few things from my family. I still remember my aunt demonstrating her favorite espionage technique. I had gotten hold of a letter sent to my boyfriend, by someone I suspected was a rival female. After delivering a stern lecture about the inappropriateness of snooping through my boyfriend's mailbox, my aunt snatched the letter away from me and, grasping it with a set of tongs, held it over a bubbling tea kettle. My aunt, the most impulsive of women, suddenly had infinite patience. . . . It took her about half an hour to steam the letter open without getting it all soggy.

After reading its contents—it turned out to be a letter from another guy who just happened to have feminine handwriting—my aunt sealed the letter back up, brought it out to the backyard, and stomped on it a few times for good measure. "There," she said, holding up her handiwork.

"The mailman must have dropped it before he delivered it. You know how careless the U.S. Postal Service is."

I was eighteen before I discovered that not everyone's family knew the best ways to steam mail, pick locks, and record telephone conversations.

✳   ✳   ✳   ✳

Ray and I had been trying to have children for a while, and one day, after my mother asked me for the two hundredth time when we were going to start a family, I confessed that we'd already been trying for a year. Little did I realize this information would quickly become my mother's most scintillating cocktail-party conversation.

The next time we were visiting friends with my mother, I was headed into the kitchen to get another glass of wine when I saw her observing my husband lovingly, and murmuring to a friend, "Look at him! So handsome! Who would ever guess his sperm count's so low?"

—Maria F., 36, restaurant owner, Chicago, Illinois

✳   ✳   ✳   ✳

This was during the sixties in the Midwest, where men were men and sheep were scared. It was also the time when men were discovering they didn't have to stick so carefully to gender roles.

That year, we had a new option for phys-ed class: folk dancing. I wanted to take it, and my father was relentless in his opposition—no son of *his* was going to do that kind of fag stuff. Baseball, football, hell, even lacrosse would have been preferable. We had a huge fight about it, and we didn't talk for weeks.

What he didn't realize was that I was one of only three straight guys in folk dancing, so I got to have sex with about half the class.

—Mark H., 44, book editor, New York, New York

* * * *

I waited until I was thirty to vote for the first time; but like many first-time voters, I was very vocal about my preference. As it happens, I was for Bill Clinton. My parents, life-long Republicans, were equally vocal about their preference for George Bush. They simply couldn't believe that in this, my first vote, I was going to "cancel out" one of their votes. We spent hours and hours and *hours* arguing. On the morning of Election Day, I made the mistake of inviting them over for breakfast. When I went to cast my vote, they insisted on following me. By the time we got to the voting booths, they were both ranting about George Bush and shouting at me like I was ten years old.

"Go ahead, vote for Clinton," my father said. "You'll get the government you deserve!"

The police at the polls decided this fight constituted "electioneering"—and I got to watch both my red-white-and-blue parents being dragged away, trying to explain to the officer that it was their daughter who was *the criminal*. . . .

—Eileen T., 32, Des Moines, Iowa

* * * *

My boyfriend is almost twenty-three years old. Since I just turned sixteen, to my parents this is sort of equivalent to finding out their daughter is romantically involved with the fat, balding boss. Still, I didn't understand why they hated him with *such* a passion, until my boyfriend told me my mother had reported him to the police, under the suspicion that he was a heroin dealer.

He happens to be diabetic, so there would always be syringes lying around our apartment. I guess I had kind of forgotten to tell her.

—Tiffany T., bartender, Decatur, Georgia

* * * *

My parents married late, and so my father was going through his second childhood while I was going through my first. So *he* was the one throwing spaghetti on the wall (to see if it was cooked properly) and making paper airplanes out of the second sheets of Mama's good stationery (an amateur pilot, he wanted to teach the laws of aerodynamics, he said). I adored him. But I still remember, when I was thirteen and wanted to get my ears pierced, we had our first big fight.

"They're my ears," I shrieked.

He pointed at them and said menacingly, "They're *my* ears until you're twenty-one."

—Abigail Z., 24, biology grad student, Madison, Wisconsin

* * * *

My mother had an uncanny instinct for knowing when I was doing something—anything—she knew I shouldn't. She always used to say, "I have eyes in the back of my head." When I was six I remember peering at her hair, trying to figure out where the eyes were and how she could see out of them.

At any rate, I still remember the first time I managed to get this girl to come over to my house. I was sixteen. It was late; my parents were asleep; the girl and I were in the bedroom. And here it was, the big moment—*I would actually get to go to second base.* For a Jewish boy from Larchmont, New York, this was a very big moment. But just at the *very* moment I had screwed up all my courage, and I was braving the "Mysteries of the Bra Hooks," I hear this tsk-tsking voice outside my door:

"No *Goodbye, Columbus* in the Federman household!"

I was too mortified to continue any further. I made the girl get up, put on her sweater, and leave.

—Manny F., 43, TV news producer, Pittsburgh, Pennsylvania

✳   ✳   ✳   ✳

My mother used to work at a drive-up-drop-off-your-film booth. Even though it was out of our way, my husband and I felt that, since she worked there, we should do business with the place. I suspected that she was looking at our pictures before she gave them back to us—no big deal—but she swore she would *never* do such a thing. In our more juvenile moods, my husband and I thought about taking pictures of ourselves naked, waiting for her to say something, etc., etc., but we controlled ourselves.

Finally, though, my suspicions were confirmed the day I received a packet of photos and found that one of them had a big, U-shaped slice cut from the center. When I asked her about it, she told me that the picture made her arm look fat, so she cut it out with a pair of scissors.

—Rita N., 33, travel agent, Dallas, Texas

✳   ✳   ✳   ✳

The first huge fight I got into with my parents as an adolescent was because I wouldn't carry around a petition for Nixon to bring back our POWs from Vietnam. I was just one of those teenagers who hated people who went to fight, as if all those clueless nineteen-year-olds were evil warmongers. My contention was, I wasn't going to embarrass myself in front of my friends by working on behalf of Nixon. My mother's contention was: We are Republicans, therefore you're a Republican, too.

That was the first time I ran away from home.

—Rachel P., 38, housewife, New York, New York

✳   ✳   ✳   ✳

My mother is an insomniac. When I was a kid, she used to clean the house all night long. She never turned on the lights in my room, so I eventually learned to sleep through it. But it got to the point where she was looking for things to do. She started "straightening" the contents of my drawers. I asked her to just leave my stuff alone, but she ignored my pleas. I got desperate. God only knows what I expected her to find, since at that point I wouldn't have known what to do with, say, a naked picture of Heather Locklear. But still, a guy needs his privacy. We lived near a five-and-dime, so I bought a dozen mousetraps and several bags of Ping-Pong balls. I cleaned out my desk drawer and set all the traps with the balls on top. When she came to clean out the drawer, all the traps went off, and the balls were flying everywhere. From my strategic location under the bed, I could see her panic and run out of the room. I thought she had learned a lesson. Unfortunately, she returned with a bucket of ice, threw back the covers, saw I wasn't there, and then tossed all the ice neatly under the bed in one swift motion.

She got her revenge, but I won the battle. She never cleaned my room again.

—Jay F., 23, computer programmer, Lansing, Michigan

✳   ✳   ✳   ✳

I was in my second year as a counselor at summer camp near my home in Arizona, and I was planning to do the unthinkable, as far as my family was concerned: I was having my boyfriend visit. This guy was a few years older than I was . . . twenty, I think. Anyway, somehow—and to this day, I don't know how—my father got wind of my plan. He managed to convince the local sheriff that this guy was plotting to kidnap a minor. Dad described my boyfriend's car, and the sheriff issued an APB for the surrounding vicinity. It must have been a slow day for the police department in Tucson, because a bunch of them actually hung around the camp, waited for my boyfriend to show up, and then took him in for questioning.

My parents had something of a kidnapping mania. I remember another time, not that long after the camp incident, when a few of my friends had planned a surprise party for my friend Nicole. The way my house was constructed, I used to enter and exit very often from my bedroom window. Anyway, on this particular night some friends had dropped by around ten P.M. and said they were there to take me to the party. So I wrote my mother a note: "I've been kidnapped; don't worry, I'll be back in a few hours." Then I climbed out the window.

I should have known that "kidnap" was a bad choice of words. Not hearing me in my room, my mother broke in with a wire hanger, found the note, and decided I'd been forced to write it by a team of guys whose role models were Harvey Keitel and Christopher Walken.

Several hours later, I returned home to find my father and two policemen searching the area for my body, and my mother, weeping and almost incoherent from tranquilizers.

—Annie D., 25, newspaper reporter, Phoenix, Arizona

✳ ✳ ✳ ✳

The first time my lover went with me to my parents' house, my mother waited until there were only the two of them in the room. Then she asked him, "Are you guys together mainly for the sex?"

I never leave my mother alone with my lover now.

—Jay, 34, housepainter, Ossining, New York

✳ ✳ ✳ ✳

I think the defining moment in my relationship with my mother came when we had our first hair fight. I was twelve. She thought my hair was too sexy when it was long, so she wanted me to wear it short. Naturally, I preferred it long. She didn't argue with me; oh, no. She just waited until I was asleep—and cut it all off.

This is the same mother who comes to my house now

and insists I'm an untidy slob because it's a form of childhood rebellion. I just turned forty.

—Pamela S., dental hygienist, Juneau, Alaska

* * * *

When I was living at home, I would frequently stay out late, drinking in bars and such. My folks never got upset about my lurching home at five in the morning. They had a much more subtle way of wreaking revenge: At 6 A.M., my mother would decide she needed to vacuum my room.

To this day, I hate vacuums.

—Roger, 44, salesman, Denver, Colorado

* * * *

I'm a lesbian; when my lover and I went to visit her mom a few years ago, she very pointedly asked us, "What do you do when you both have your periods?"

Gail looked as if she wanted to sink into the earth. I quickly told her mom, "We take lots of Midol and say really bitchy things to each other."

—Sherry T., 28, government employee, Tallahassee, Florida

* * * *

Words of (Dubious) Wisdom: "Take My Advice"

Remember all those warm parent-child bonding moments on television commercials? The one where dad hands his boy a Lifesaver and passes along the fly-fishing metaphor that encompasses everything he's learned about life?

Interesting, isn't it, that much of the advice your parents gave you, you've spent the rest of your life trying desperately to unlearn.

* * * *

My mother lived by an interesting credo she tried to instill in me from the time I was a young girl. It began the day I got my period: She handed me ten bucks and told me a woman should always get money for being a woman.

Because that's how she lived her life. Mother was an extraordinarily beautiful woman who had been the mistress of many powerful men. (I was adopted, because she wanted a

child but she didn't want to ruin her figure with a preg-
nancy.) It was the custom in Hong Kong, where we came
from, that every time a man would tire of their relationship,
he would give her a house. My mother had twelve houses.
And as she grew older, she became more and more of a
dowager empress.

After I came to America, I had one relationship after the
other; I would tell my mother about them, and she was always appalled—not by the fact that the relationships ended,
but about how I mismanaged the potential advantages. Her
usual response when another affair had gone belly-up:
"What! And you did not even get a house?"

—Lee T., 35, marketing executive, San Francisco, California

✳   ✳   ✳   ✳

My mother runs a wire service for hypochondriacs: Every
week she'll save health-related clippings from the daily paper and tell me what insidious disease I have to beware of
this week. I was out all day yesterday, and this is what I
found when I came back to my answering machine:

"Jane, there's been an outbreak of E. coli in parts of
the water system in New York City. Boil your water."
Beep

"Jane, remember, last week was your thirty-fifth birthday, so please make sure you call your gynecologist and
make an appointment for a mammogram." **Beep**

"Jane, I forgot to tell you, there was an article this
week that says caffeine is *not* linked to kidney problems,
as I previously reported. But I think you should still cut
down to one cup a day." **Beep**

"Jane, the *New York Times* says every man over fifty

should have yearly digital rectal exams and a new blood-antigen test that allows doctors to catch prostate cancer early." **Beep**

"Jane, you can disregard that last message. I hit the wrong speed-dial number. That was for your uncle."

—Jane H., 35, freelance writer, New York, New York

✳ ✳ ✳ ✳

My mother and father didn't like us to know that they didn't have the answers to everything—they preferred to remain invincible gods. So they would come up with answers to any question my brothers and I could think up. One day while driving to my grandparents' house, we asked our parents: Where do all those pieces of tires lying on the side of the road come from?

Without missing a beat, my mother informed us they were dead tires that had been cut off of truckers' teams of tires—sort of like a dog sled. Driving through the central valley of California in summertime, you see great plumes of dust. These, she told us, are the dust trails from the packs of wild tires that roam the valley. Back in the old days, the great tirehunters—like Goodyear, Michelin, and others—cut down the vast herds and domesticated some. Soon a rich and prosperous trade was born. Great ranches of tires grew in the larger western states. (Tires need a lot of room to grow.) But still the hunters went out and clubbed baby tires to get the treads to make sandals with.

Nowadays the wild tires are threatened; the federal government is considering putting them on the endangered-species list. Sometimes wild tires will attack domesticated tires on empty stretches of road, causing them to go flat.

Truckers sometimes have problems with one of their pack going feral and attacking its running mate. That's why, on the top of a steep grade, you see them pounding on the tires with a club, to make sure the tires don't attack each other. They are dangerous critters when aroused, so when you're changing a flat be careful, and watch the teeth.

To this day, I feel especially brave when I'm changing a tire.

—Harold G., 40, psychiatrist, Los Angeles, California

* * * *

Recently I found a paper I wrote in the seventh grade on feminism—this was in 1974—and I realized just how many of these bizarre mixed messages came directly from my mother:

"Women's Lib was formed because women would really like to get out of the habit of being used as sex objects and prostitutes";

"Women who want to be successful with men should be quiet, and let the male be dominant."

"Women should pretend they're not as smart as men, even though they are smarter."

"Men believe women are most valued for their looks, which usually ends up with a woman getting some sort of venereal disease."

—Adele S., 33, homemaker, Chicago, Illinois

* * * *

My folks, particularly my mom, are as loony, neurotic, and irrational as anyone else's. But I must say they always had my best interests in mind. At least, that's what they always told me as they twisted my mind and scarred my psyche forever.

Throughout my life, whenever I brought my troubles to my dad, he always listened carefully and then delivered this piece of wisdom: "Things have a way of working out one way or another." It wasn't until I was thirty-three or so that I realized this nugget, which I had always cherished and quoted to others, was totally devoid of any content at all. In effect what he was saying was, "Something will happen. It doesn't matter what it is; it will happen and you'll be stuck with it." Must be his Russian heritage.

Oh, well. Who knows what my kids will say about me? They're already headed down Dysfunction Turnpike.

—Ed S., 38, professor of sociology, Omaha, Nebraska

✳   ✳   ✳   ✳

My favorite piece of advice from Dad was, "You'd be such a pretty girl if you'd only keep your mouth shut."

—Anne S., 39, guidance counselor, San Diego, California

✳   ✳   ✳   ✳

My best friend's mother went through a painful divorce when my friend was twelve, and I think it unhinged her. About a month after their dad left the house, each of the six kids had this little ritual they had to perform in the morning: Before they could open the refrigerator door, they had to recite this saying she had pinned up on the door with a refrigerator magnet: WOMEN NEED MEN AS MUCH AS ELEPHANTS NEED BICYCLES. Even the boys in the family had to say it.

At the time, we thought Ally's mom was sort of kooky; in retrospect, she needed serious help. I remember one day Ally and I decided to play hookey from school. We were the kind of painfully dull good girls whose idea of an exciting adventure was to skip school, stay home, and bake cookies.

But when Ally's mother found out we hadn't been in school, she immediately called my parents and told them *we were running a prostitution ring*. (Remember, this was before anyone had heard of Amy Fisher, so prostitution would not be the career most mothers would immediately have thought of for their truant children.) My mother was shocked Ally's mother could even think of her daughter that way. And me? Well, at this point, I'd never even been out on a date.

Ally's mom also used to play tennis. In our neighborhood, all the moms played tennis, but Ally's mom became very good very fast. One day, I asked her how she improved so rapidly. She replied, "I've started to think of the tennis balls as my children's heads."

—Eliza D., 30, paralegal, Valley Stream, New York

✳   ✳   ✳   ✳

Throughout my childhood, if I lost something and asked Mom if she knew where it was, her answer was always the same: "It's where you put it last." It took me until I was about twelve years old to figure out I was being had.

—Mary A., 34, homemaker, Gary, Indiana

✳   ✳   ✳   ✳

Signs *That I'm Becoming My Own Father:*

1. I actually said to my son the other day, *"I'll* give you something to cry about!"
2. Worse, I heard myself saying the one thing my dad *always* used to say to me when I headed off to Scout camp, college, or any other extended trip—and *always* in the presence of my peers:

   "Remember you're a Finkelman!"

   —Ted F., 38, internist, Hicksville, New York

*   *   *   *

I was in the hospital after having a hysterectomy. My husband Sam had just left when my mother walked in the door. She took my hand lovingly and said, "Darling, now that you're half a woman, you've got to face the possibility Sam will look elsewhere for satisfaction."

   —Martha, C., 43, Lansing, Michigan

*   *   *   *

My mother is famous for using language that only she can understand. Rather, she has a way of mating two pieces of advice together, to make it her own. Her most recent: Apparently she was trying to tell us, "Don't talk with your mouth full" or "Don't chew with your mouth open." Instead, she yelled, "Don't talk with your mouth open!" My mother has developed quite a reputation for this. Usually, only my grandmother—her mother—has been able to decipher the code, as she is known for the same speech impediment. My sister recently finished a sentence for our mother, and this caused her great distress. I believe her exact words were, "My God, I understood her."

—Brad D., 17, high-school student, Milwaukee, Wisconsin

* * * *

My mother is one of those people who did not believe in giving her children hang-ups, as she calls them; consequently, I'm one of the most prudish people you'll ever meet. But at any rate, her favorite saying to me was, "I'm not your mother. I'm your friend."

One day, in a moment of pique, I had to tell her the truth: "Look, if you weren't my mother, you'd never be my friend."

—Lana S., set designer, Austin, Texas

* * * *

My mother's favorite expression: "The screwing you're getting isn't worth the screwing you're getting." Then she wonders why I'm thirty-five and still single.

—Amy S., 35, bank manager, New York, New York

* * * *

"Never eat when you're not hungry." That was always the advice my mother gave us about weight control. Yet a typical Saturday breakfast in my house consisted of pancakes or "hockies," which were fried bread dough lathered with butter. We'd have contests to see who could eat the most. The candy jar was always filled with lollipops and chocolates, which we weren't supposed to touch because they were fattening. I wanted to take ballet lessons, which would have helped me slim down, but I was told I was "too fat" to take them . . . but here, honey, a cookie will make you feel better.

Even today, I still have a serious weight problem. I still get a hard time for being so fat, and my mother is still making my favorite foods and saying, "I know you shouldn't eat this but . . ." Or she makes them for my kids, while saying to me, "Now, Cathy, don't *you* eat any of this. . . ."

The *lightest* of us five kids weighs 250 pounds. . . .

—Cathy O., 40, homemaker, Des Moines, Iowa

* * * *

Here was some advice from Mom that really came in handy: When I was fifteen, she sat me down and said, "Remember, when a girl tells you 'No,' she really means 'Yes.' "

Luckily, my new girlfriend at the time was stronger than I, and she set me straight on this issue. That first time I thought her "No" meant "Yes," I ended up in a cast.

—Bill J., 22, security officer, Toronto, Canada

* * * *

When I turned thirteen and got my period, my mother, who came from Russia, informed me, "If you touch a plant during your time of the month, that plant will wither and die." She also told me there was no such thing as PMS or menstrual cramps; when a woman had those problems, she had something on her conscience.

I believed both of these things until I was twenty. By the time I discovered they weren't necessarily true—I could have PMS and I wasn't particularly guilty about *anything*—I was in my junior year at college. At that point, I went out and bought all these plants, and my room looked like a greenhouse.

—Tanya T., 39, economics professor, Chicago, Illinois

*   *   *   *

Every week my mother sends me nutrition articles, articles about breast cancer, lung cancer, new feminine cancers you've never even heard of. During a particularly difficult period of my life, I was in the hospital being treated for clinical depression. I had been there for only about a week, when my mother came in with a recent article she'd clipped on cancer and secondary smoke.

Apparently she didn't feel I had enough to worry about.

—Elaine L., 30, writer, New York, New York

*   *   *   *

When I was a little girl and I was upset, my mother's response to every problem would be, "Don't cry. Here's a cookie." There were five us at home, and she always carried them with her.

Recently she was over at my house and I started to tell her about a fight I'd had with my husband, and I got kind of teary—something I hadn't done in front of her in a long, long time. She reached into her bag and handed me a cookie. I'm thirty years old. And you know what? The cookie still helps.

—Faye D., 30, clothing designer, Keene, New Hampshire.

*   *   *   *

The Frugal Parent

Who says they can't take it with them?

* * * *

My parents took only one vacation a year together without us: a long weekend away at a convention at a resort center. This particular year, they were a bit hard up for money—and we had ruled out all the inexpensive baby-sitters they would have considered. There were three of us girls—ten, seven, and three. I was the oldest. We are Catholic, and we lived in a closely knit parish. My mother reportedly called the parish office to get some other names to try out as a baby-sitter. Then, some genius at the parish suggested she put us at the orphanage for a few days. As I remember, the selling points were that we'd be with other kids (undoubtedly projected as incredible fun) and that the orphans were at the summer orphanage—sort of a big camp with a swimming pool, ponies, the whole bit. At any rate, my parents felt Catholics in the same parish wouldn't lie to one another, so this analysis was trusted. The reservation was made, and we packed our little bags.

At this point in my memory, things become a little fuzzy. I *do* remember that the ponies, seasoned beasts that they were, both kicked and bit, and no one could get close to them. Also, since it was the first week the "summer orphanage" was open, the pool was still closed. So it was the orphans' job to clean out the winter muck from the uncovered swamp they called a pool. And we were on the muck team.

And then there were the long rows of bunks with wailing children—and *weird* children. Remember, these were the days of real orphanages—kids left in baskets outside doors, dour nuns, that sort of thing. What I mostly remember was that the bathrooms were so horrific I decided early on that they were too dirty for anything that seriously required sitting down. Therefore, I stopped going to the bathroom—a stand that seriously altered my perceptions of how much fun the weekend was.

My then-seven-year-old sister also remembers this: When we arrived, she told the first little kid who came up to her that our parents had just dropped us off for the weekend.

"That's funny," the little girl said. "My mother told me that, too . . . three years ago."

—Betsy A., 46, homemaker, Montclair, New Jersey

✳   ✳   ✳   ✳

My mother lived through the Depression, so I guess it's understandable that every time she heard the word *recession* she'd sort of panic. During the Carter years, during the

'90–'91 Bush years ... during these periods, my mother would go into canning mode. For some reason, she thought the food item that she'd need most when the next Great Depression hit was pickled eggs. We had, literally, an entire basement filled with these things. I'm still eating pickled eggs from 1973.

Mom also washed used Saran Wrap and tin foil, which I guess isn't that unusual. But I remember watching her spend *hours* repairing twisties, taping up those little pieces of wire so she could reuse them. ...

—Noreen O., 43, police officer, Portland, Oregon

✳   ✳   ✳   ✳

My first year of college at a local state school in the mid-sixties was pretty cheap: Selling my stereo and comic-book collection paid for tuition. But that didn't leave me enough to live on. So I took out a student loan for $1,500. What I did was, I got the loan check, cashed the money, and gave it to my parents; I asked them to hold it for me and send me about two hundred dollars a month. I wanted to make sure I didn't suddenly lose my mind and blow the money on the horses or something.

Anyway, when I went to school, I took about enough money to get me through the first two months. I called the 'rents and asked for money; they said it wasn't available, and we would talk about it at Christmas.

Before Christmas break, I was pretty close to broke, so I had to hitchhike home. I told them again I needed some more money. They just said, "We had to use it."

Now you have to understand, my parents are very solidly upper-middle class. But their response to me was, "Do you know how much money we spent raising you?" Not only did I have to drop out of the second semester, but ultimately, *I had to pay back the loan.*

At the time, however, I didn't make a big fuss; given the family I grew up in, it seemed perfectly understandable that my parents would spend my college tuition money. I asked that since I couldn't go back to college for a while, would they mind if I moved back home? Well, they preferred that I didn't, but . . .

It took a great deal of persuading, but finally my mother let me move into the kennel—she was breeding teacup toy poodles—so I consigned to live with these sinister little mutants and clean their shit every day.

What can I say? She was going through menopause at the time, and she was just wacky.

—George G., 43, editor, New York, New York

✳ ✳ ✳ ✳

Mom was cheap, she but also lacked common sense. She was the kind of person who would spend twenty-nine cents to send me a twenty-cents-off coupon on Tide. Money, she felt, was a perfectly good excuse for anything, even (maybe especially) enduring various forms of misery.

For example, my sister was desperate to extract herself from her marriage. The degree of her desperation can be gauged by the fact that she had four children, ages five to fourteen, and she *still* wanted a divorce; she was enrolled in some sort of program that has since made her the head of a mental ward at a New York metropolitan-area hospital. But when she called my mother to break the news, the conversation went like this:

My sister: Mother, I can't stand him, I can't go on living with him, I've got to get a divorce.

Mother: Don't be silly, dear. He's a *doctor*.

—Ruth D., 39, furniture designer, Arlington, Virginia

* * * *

I remember most vividly the road trips with my parents and my older brother. Naturally, he always got to sleep on the backseat, and I was relegated to the floor, which on a '67 Olds had a tremendously huge transmission hump. No wonder I have a bad back to this day.

My mother and father always wanted to save every dime possible, so they searched out and found the cheapest motel in every hole-in-the-wall town we stayed in. But even though the hotels were cheap and a little sleazy, my mother always came prepared. She was the "advance" team, much like the Secret Service. She would go in and "sweep" the room (literally and figuratively), spraying phone, bedding, chairs, lamps, TV (if there was one), toilets, faucets, tub, shower head, tile floors, and closets with Lysol. We never had to worry about falling asleep later that night—the fumes took care of that.

When I grew up, I vowed I'd never be such a penny-pincher. Of course, the moral to this story is that, even though I now make over a hundred thousand dollars a year, I have such huge expenses I'm still somehow living hand to mouth, while my parents tool up and down the West Coast in their beautiful forty-foot motor home.

—Jed Y., 32, lawyer, Muncie, Indiana

* * * *

My mother, though I love her dearly, is something of an airhead. Combine this with her almost pathological cheapness, and you've got an endless series of family fiascos.

We grew up in a prefab house (circa 1953), and standard operating procedure after using the toilet was to stand up, flush, and watch the water rise in the bowl. If the water rose above a certain level, it was almost certain to overflow unless one grabbed the plunger and started to work right away.

One afternoon my dad was following SOP, when it became obvious he would need the plunger; however, my mother had reorganized the bathroom and the plunger was nowhere to be found. So my panic-stricken father yelled, "Mona, where's the plunger?"

To which my mother replied, "It's in the medicine cabinet."

Now, this cabinet was about eighteen inches wide, and none of the shelves was more than six inches deep. Not exactly a lot of space for a toilet plunger. So my father, now with wet feet, yelled back, "It can't be in the cabinet. It won't fit."

Mom's answer: "I know! I had to break the handle off."

So for about the next three months, we were using an eight-inch-handled toilet plunger made for midgets; we were all too afraid to ask her for money for a new one.

—Marcus L., 42, architect, Sarasota, Florida

✳   ✳   ✳   ✳

Until recently, my father had not been to a restaurant for twenty years. Whenever my mother or I would suggest going out, he would sit down with his calculator—he's an engineer—and prove to me how a fifteen dollar meal in a restaurant really costs fifty-seven cents if we bought it in the A&P—missing the point, of course, that just once in a while it would be nice for someone else to do the cooking.

Now that my siblings and I are out of the house, my mother has gotten sick of his cheapness. She has an acquaintance who works as a waitress at a local restaurant, and she got this friend to agree to play along with this little ruse: Using her computer, my mother made up a reasonable facsimile of the restaurant's menu and put prices on it from about 1960. She has actually convinced my father that there happens to be one restaurant in town that has a T-bone steak for three bucks. He'll see this menu; my mother will insist on paying the bill, and my father feels satisfied they're getting a fair price.

My mom doesn't push her luck with this one; they only go to this place once in a while, and only when she knows her friend's on duty to give Dad his "special" menu. Given the prices, Dad often wonders why this restaurant doesn't do a better business.

—Brandi A., 24, travel agent, Memphis, Tennessee

* * * *

My parents thought television was one of the great evils. They only bought a TV in 1959, on the pretext that they needed to hear the Kennedy/Nixon debates. It was always locked in their room; we had to sneak in to watch Rocky and Bullwinkle. Over the years, the TV deteriorated, and a windstorm knocked down the roof antenna. But they were scared to have anyone go up on the roof, because it might knock down the shingles. So we got only two stations for many, many years. We were all crying for our parents to put in cable, but they staunchly refused: *that* would entail drilling a hole through the side of the house. This sounds reasonable, except for the fact that the house is riddled with termites, because our folks thought exterminators were "frivolous."

Anyway, my parents finally bought a color TV and hooked it up to a wire that leads nowhere. There is virtually no reception whatsoever. But that does not prevent them from watching PBS for hours on end. Hours in front of the snow. Apparently you don't have to actually *see* the talking heads on PBS to appreciate them.

I think part of the problem is that my dad is a nice Jewish boy transplanted to Indiana from New York City, and he can't grasp the concept that anything he wants done to the house, he has to pay for: He was always waiting for the super to drop by! Waiting for, oh, about twenty years. (He heard of someone who got his arm chopped off with a power mower—which is why we have a wildlife refuge where the front lawn should be.)

He also can't get it through his head that, although he's now thousands of miles away from his old neighborhood, a desperate crackhead is *not* lurking outside the door. I mean, here he is in hick fucking Bloomington, and he spends half his life prowling around, locking the doors, hermetically sealing the house.

—Michael G., 40, book editor, Newburyport, Massachusetts

✳   ✳   ✳   ✳

When I was a young teenager in San Diego, my mother took my little brother and sister back east to her parents', leaving my other sister and myself with Dad. Dad's not big on cooking or housekeeping—and when he was alone, he could indulge in his own cheapness mania. For ten days we lived off cereal, bologna sandwiches, frozen burritos, corned beef hash, and canned tomatoes. When the meals were concluded, Dad would wipe the dishes and pots clean with a rag; soap and water were too wasteful (and let's not even talk about the dishwasher . . .). He would also make us stick to the same few dishes over and over again; using clean dishes would also be "wasteful."

About a week into this routine, Dad announced we were going out to dinner. My sister and I were thrilled—real food on clean dishes! We piled into the car, stopping to pick up our stepbrother and stepsister, then we headed to the local supermarket. At that point, my sister and I looked at each other with dread. While he cruised the aisles, Dad ate a few grapes and some fresh pea pods; I was sure we were about to be arrested. He then bought a long Gallo salami and a bottle of Gatorade. Then we drove up to a parking lot that had a lovely view of San Diego, and all five of us gnawed off the salami and swigged out of the Gatorade bottle. By the time there was about two inches of warm Gatorade left, none of us could bear to drink from it, since bits of salami were floating about in it. Dad screamed at us for being such "spoiled brats."

No kid was ever so happy to see his mom come home, and I swore that day I'd learn how to cook for myself.

—Ray F., 30, chef, Tallahassee, Florida

✳   ✳   ✳   ✳

My mom is from hell sometimes. One time we were in a parking lot, and she asked if I had a dollar, and would I pay it for parking and she'd pay me back. Well, I paid for parking, and later when I asked her for my dollar, she said, "Tough."

—Jerry W., 11, elementary-school student, Lansing, Michigan

✳   ✳   ✳   ✳

My parents' favorite threat has always been disinheritance, which really doesn't hold much weight when you're, say, seven. Given my limited grasp of finance at that time, they would have been much better off telling me I couldn't have a dollar than that I couldn't have their entire fortune; a buck, at least, I could understand.

They were forever threatening to leave their money to various people—usually my dread cousin Lynn, who at the age of seven really *did* understand the implications of inheritance. (She's since become—no kidding—a lawyer specializing in estates.)

They'd also threaten to leave their money to various causes, their favorite one being the state of Israel. "We're going to plant trees in Israel with our money if you don't shape up!" I remember my father screaming. Finally, when I was about fourteen and starting to worry about this stuff a bit, I called the Israeli embassy to see if trees really could grow in the desert. They could. They sent me a pamphlet about irrigation and grapefruits. For a while I was very upset, both for myself and the Chosen Land: I imagined Israel's entire agricultural economy was dependent on the existence of surly, misbehaved American teenagers.

These days, my parents still threaten, but the benefactor of their largesse will be their beloved granddaughter—my daughter. And, you know, that's just fine by me.

—Rachel D., 34, public-relations executive, Roslyn, New York

✳   ✳   ✳   ✳

I turned sixteen during the summer, and like most normal teenagers, I had an immediate yearning to get behind the wheel of an automobile. So that summer I took all the driver's-ed classes, watched endless hours of car movies intended to scare the bejesus out of us before we got behind the wheel, and logged in several stressful hours in the car with Mom or Dad clutching the armrest for dear life. They had a new Caddy, which they would not let me near, but they let me practice on their ancient Oldsmobile. For this kindness, they expected me to be grateful. But again and again I explained that I really shouldn't be driving the Olds—*nobody* should be driving it, except maybe Evel Knievel out for a thrill. The car was scary. But all they knew was, it was old and not worth much. Therefore, it was mine.

Anyway, summer was almost over, and we decided that I had had enough practice. It was time to take the dreaded behind-the-wheel exam. Since we lived in a large city (Dallas) at the time and since it was often difficult to get even a test appointment, we decided to spend the night with my grandparents, who lived about a half hour north of us.

The night before the test, we went up there. The next morning, while I was eating breakfast, my mom went to the DPS office to schedule my exam appointment. Well, after making the appointment, she left the office to come back home. But as she was walking to the Olds, she noticed smoke coming up from under the hood. She opened the hood, and the engine burst into flames.

This created a great deal of smoke, attracting the attention of the firemen at the station, which was across the street. So Mom screams and shouts, "Come on over! My car's on fire!"

"We can't!" the firemen yell. "You've got to call us first."

So Mom runs inside, dials 911. The siren goes off across the street, and all the firemen get into their suits, get in their fire truck, turn on the bells, and drive across the street.

Needless to say, my grandparents and I soon received a telephone call, and we immediately hurried over. But when we got there, we found another surprise. The firemen easily put out the fire. But by the time they were done, a policeman had arrived and, along with one of the firemen, was taking a look at the engine to try and determine what had gone wrong. (It was an electrical problem.) Well, the hood on this car was one of those ones that had a spring on it—not one of the kind where you had to prop the hood on a stick. What neither of the two men realized is that the spring acts strangely under conditions of high heat. So when the fireman let go of the hood—assuming it would stay up—it didn't. It hit the cop on the head. *He* had to be taken to the hospital and given stitches, and no one got to take their driver's test that day because of our crappy old Oldsmobile.

So, insisting I drive the cheap car cost Dad about eight hundred dollars in medical bills.

—Jim T., 24, sanitation worker, Kansas City, Kansas

✳   ✳   ✳   ✳

You name it, my dad is cheap about it. I grew up with a sign in our bathroom that said: "Using any more than two squares of toilet paper is WASTEFUL." His tightwaddery knew no bounds: He made us reuse dental floss and vacuum-cleaner bags; he unplugged all electrical gadgets in the house when they weren't in use; we were not allowed to have night-lights, even when we were afraid of the dark.

There was only one object my father ever bought that he claimed was worth the money. This was when he was sixty-six and planning to marry his (twenty-five-year-old), fourth wife. He had had a bit of a problem with drinking and this heart medication he took ... so he got a penile implant. Things were permanently semierect. *That*, he felt, was value on the dollar.

—Ingrid H., 41, psychoanalyst, New York, New York

✳   ✳   ✳   ✳

Miscellaneous Humiliations (From Your Cradle to Their Grave)

There are people in this world who are beyond shame; unfortunately, these people are your parents. Feeling humiliated was such a daily occurrence in my household that I just assumed everybody had parents who Xeroxed copies of their daughter's report card and sent them to relatives at Christmas. Probably the phrase my father said to me most often as I was growing up was: "Stop being soooo sensitive."

So these are what I call the toe curlers: Experiences so embarrassing your toes just automatically go into spasm at the very thought.

*   *   *   *

I was twelve years old and visiting my aunt in Malibu. I had been swimming by myself in the ocean for a couple of hours, just enjoying the time away from my folks. I got out of the water and attempted to change out of the cut-offs I'd been swimming in, into some dry clothing. But something was stuck. Real stuck. My dick was caught in the zipper. I tried *everything* to get it out, but it was caught. Finally, in embarrassment and desperation, I went back to my aunt's house and confessed what was wrong. Alarmed, she drove me to the nearest emergency room. The doctor on call shot novocaine into my penis and then told me he'd have to do a little operation—but he needed the permission of one of my parents. My mother was a few hours away, in San Diego, so my aunt gave him her number.

Now up till this point, I was embarrassed but stoic; at twelve, I was determined to be a man. I wasn't going to get rattled over every little thing. But as I stood there, the zipper hanging off my increasingly numb weenie, I overheard the doctor talking to my mother: "It's not that funny, ma'am. Please. Stop. It's not funny."

At which point, I just burst into tears. I cried and cried. I couldn't believe it. I felt totally betrayed.

Years later, every time I mentioned this story, she would start giggling uncontrollably. My mother died last year, and I told the story at her funeral. I know she still would have laughed.

—Roger J., television reporter, New York, New York

* * * *

At fifty-seven, my mother is still trying to find herself. This latest scheme is something she cooked up with her best friend, Lee, a Chinese woman with blond hair, a boob lift, and a nose job. This is a woman whose picture you'll find if you look in the dictionary under "identity crisis." Anyway, she and Lee have decided to write a book about masturbation. My mother seems to enjoy discussing her plan for this book in front of my new husband—she'll go on and on about how important this subject is in the age of AIDS, etc., etc. And the thing I have nightmares about is *maybe this book will get off the ground*. My mother, everywhere I turn! The masturbation specialist!

Fortunately, though, her interests seem to be changing somewhat. I talked to her yesterday, and she told me she's going to become a rune therapist. This is someone who apparently reads people's rocks.

—Lacey D., 34, graphic designer, Dallas, Texas

* * * *

My parents divorced when I was twelve. I still remember one of the last fights they had—Mom screaming that Dad did nothing to help her around the house, then Dad flinging all the food from the refrigerator around the kitchen. It was the biggest food fight I'd ever seen. I still remember Mom jumping up and down on a loaf of bread.

Anyway, I went to live with my father. When I went to visit my mom and we went out together, she made me introduce herself to people as her *friend*—because God forbid anyone know she had a daughter as old as I was.

—Samantha J., 27, flight attendant, San Diego, California

* * * *

When I was little and about ready to enter school, Mom decided it was time to give up Bah-Bah, my beloved blanket, which I held tightly in my fist, the rest of it draped over the top of my hand so I could smell it as I sucked my thumb. That summer before kindergarten, Mom would inform me on a fairly regular basis that Bah-Bah was dirty and needed to be washed. It would return cleaner but . . . smaller. She did this repeatedly until Bah-Bah went to the laundry room and never came back. *Sniff.*

About two decades later, I put two and two together (okay, so I was slow). Turned out my mom was cutting around the perimeter of Bah-Bah until Bah-Bah was no more. She thought this was a better approach than simply being honest.

—Lise D., 33, therapist, Chicago, Illinois

* * * *

I've always had a strange group of friends. However, sometimes I think my parents work hard on trying to match them in strangeness. Some of my friends from college and I were in the house, discussing how various people resembled their families. My mom then said, "Yes, and he's going to be bald, just like his father." She then grabbed me by the neck, bent me over in a hammer-lock, and pointed out to my friends just where I was going to go bald. Of course, the guys were delighted. One of them dryly remarked afterward, "So, does she show your bald spot to everyone, or just for special occasions?"

Incidentally, I do not yet have a bald spot. Really.

—Bernie S., 22, college student, Omaha, Nebraska

* * * *

My sister lived in Japan for a year, on one of those foreign-exchange programs. When she came back, a kid from the Japanese family came to live with us. His name was Jidai (pron. Hee-day), and my mother never, ever got the name right. No matter how many times we told her, the name would come out Ji-dye, or Ju-do, or some such variation. Of course, the Japanese are so excruciatingly polite, they'll never correct you. In fact, later I learned that when my sister was in Japan, she didn't know that the word for *urinal* is very similar to "you're welcome"—so the family *she* lived with allowed her to answer every "thank you" with "urinal" for a whole year.

—Jesse G., 25, hotel administrator, Honolulu, Hawaii

✳   ✳   ✳   ✳

I was in eighth grade, and our high-school basketball team was off to the regional playoffs. We travelled some miles to play. We lost in the last ten seconds.

When I got home, there were poster boards set up on chairs in the kitchen. The first had a crude drawing of me saying: "Bye, Mom, I'm off to the big game!" The second said: "Who could lose a game in the last ten seconds? Harold! That's who!" The next board had another drawing of me with tears falling and me saying: "Boo-hoo." Sitting on the last chair was a makeshift dummy stabbing itself in the chest with a knife, complete with fake blood made with food coloring. The sign around its neck said: "Harold."

Some mothers bake cookies; others knit, crochet, or throw pots. My mom spent hours creating that little display. And people wonder why I have the sense of humor I do.

—Harold M., 24, computer analyst, Secaucus, New Jersey

* * * *

My father has never been the most tactful of men. Recently my dad, his brother, and his brother's wife—all avid poker players—were deeply involved in a game with several friends. The hand was dealt. My uncle picked his cards up, looked at them, and promptly keeled over with a heart attack. They called EMS but, in the process of trying to revive him, knocked over the card table.

My dad waited till he got to the funeral to go over to his sister-in-law, the bereaved widow, who was weeping over the casket. "Tell me," he said gently, "what kind of hand did he have?"

—Timothy L., 45, hardware-store owner, Miami, Florida

* * * *

My mother's favorite hobby is sending stuff back in restaurants. But it wasn't enough for her to send her dish back— she liked to insist we send ours back, too, whether or not we liked it.

Last week my sister and I were with her in a fancy New York restaurant when my mother complained about the meat being underdone. She said my sister Jan's dish was underdone, too, even though my sister liked her meat rare. She motioned the waiter over, complained loudly, and despite my sister's protestations ordered the waiter to take *her* dish. Jan held on to her plate politely but firmly. My mother told the waiter if he didn't take Jan's plate and cook the meat she wasn't going to pay for it. Finally, my sister picked up her steak knife and said, "Mother, if you don't shut up, I'm going to have to stab you."

Mother shut up for six months. She literally refused to say a word to either of us.

—Marcy A., 36, literary agent, Brooklyn, New York

＊　＊　＊　＊

My father was a mechanic, and one day when I was thirteen I had been boasting about my dad to this girl I was trying to impress. She told me her typewriter was broken; could my father fix it? Piece of cake, I said.

So my father came over, and within the space of half an hour he had every key and moving part on the machine scattered around the room. It was at that point I noticed the travel-lock on the typewriter was on. I put the lock in the "Off" position, and the thing immediately started to work.

Well, it *would* have worked if my father could have figured out how to put it back together properly. By this time, the typewriter was scrap metal. The girl was so mad she never talked to me for the remainder of the school year.

That's when I learned where I inherited one of my most endearing characteristics: the ability to overlook the obvious, easy solution to any problem.

—Bob D., 28, investment banker, New York, New York

＊　＊　＊　＊

Mom was an avid gardener. She had this one plant she was particularly fond of, a camellia bush. I don't know why she loved it so . . . maybe because she started growing it from a twiglet, and being a slow-growing sort of plant, it was still just a tiny thing after five years. But in its effort to grow at all, it had put much of its energy that year into producing one very long branch that threw off its symmetry.

Mom asked me to get the clippers and trim it. I wanted to play baseball with the kids down the street. She insisted, somewhat testily. I resisted at first but finally fetched the clippers and trimmed the bush approximately a half inch from the ground. End of camellia project.

Mom chased me around the house with a broom, yelling curses I didn't even know she knew in Italian. I ran with my hands over my head, warding off the blows and shouting, "Forgive me!" But she never did. Forty years have passed. Unfortunately, she's somewhat confused, and we had to put her in a nursing home. Last week I visited her, and the first thing she did when she saw me was shake her finger at me accusingly and hiss, "What did you do to my camellia?"

—Anthony L., 50, building contractor, Bronx, New York

✳   ✳   ✳   ✳

When I was a teenager, I had a thing about eating in front of boys—it wasn't ladylike, and I thought that for a boy to like me he had to think of me as a delicate flower; after all, aren't all heroines in romances fragile little things?

Of course, my mother knew how I felt. Yet the first time I brought a boy home and we were making pleasant chit-chat, he said something about how I hadn't been hungry at dinner. My mother boomed, "My daughter, not hungry? Are you kidding? Why, we had to put a lock on our refrigerator!"

As you can imagine, the charming image of me having to be forcibly restrained from eating myself into a stupor was enough to make me avoid that guy for the rest of the school year.

—Elsa D., 29, poet, Seattle, Washington

✳   ✳   ✳   ✳

My father will show off his collection of fighter-pilot helmets at the, well, at the drop of a hat. At my eleventh birthday, my father stole the show by modelling thirty-two of the helmets in his collection. Homicide would have been too good for him at that point. The worst one has built-in goggles that make him look like a giant insect.

—Randy Y., 12, junior-high-school student, Putney, Vermont

✳   ✳   ✳   ✳

I was going to a football game with some friends at college. Since one of my friends was black, my father insisted on going with us so no one would see me sitting with a black man. He seated me on one end of the bench and sat next to me; my black friend Chad was about five people down.

My friend got his revenge, though. He invited my family over to what he called a block party at his house; Chad lives in an almost all-white neighborhood, so Dad thought he was being a big, progressive-minded man by going to the party. What Chad didn't mention to my father was that the party was really a birthday celebration for Chad's little nephew. My dad was the only white guy there. Chad sat Dad next to one of his uncles, a professor at a black university, and a Muslim who just happens to believe in black separatism. You can pretty much imagine what a rollicking good time the two of them had.

Susie T., 20, college student, Birmingham, Alabama

* * * *

My mother and father are convinced that one of their most important roles as parents is to help me purchase clothes, and they have not wavered in that belief since I graduated from college.

Problem is, the only person in the world who has worse taste in clothing than me is my mother—only I have the sense to know I don't have any taste, and she doesn't. She would select things and, given a few hours and a few little words of encouragement ("Try this on" and "This is perfect for you"), turn me into a complete and utter dork. I still remember being forced to wear this fisherman's mesh T-shirt, which my mother said was "cute," but which, with my red hair and complexion, made me look like a lobster caught in a net.

—Jake S., 29, restaurant manager, Baltimore, Maryland

* * * *

My father was a textbook hypochondriac; *The Merck Manual* was his bible. What I remember most vividly was this period he went through when he insisted on wearing a crash helmet. He'd wear it to the mall, he'd wear it to PTA meetings—*everywhere.* Apparently he had decided that he was getting an earache because of the draft from the car's open window. But even driving with the air conditioner off and the windows closed, in the middle of a humid Houston summer, was not enough—he *still* was sure he'd get sick.

I remember lying down on the backseat of the car when he took me to school. I didn't want to run into anyone I knew while a balding man in a crash helmet was driving me around, going fifteen miles an hour.

—Mary Jo B., car dealer, Atlanta, Georgia

✳ ✳ ✳ ✳

For my first dance at junior high, Mom dressed me in a pastel-blue pullover sweater and a white shirt with one of those Western string ties, dress slacks . . . and white socks. We lived in southern New Jersey in the sixties—*nobody* wore white socks with black shoes. It was traumatic. To this day, I only wear black socks. No brown. No navy. Black. (It makes matching the lone socks easier after washing.)

You know how people have that dream where they find themselves back at school, without any clothes on? Well, to this day, my version of that dream is that *I'm in school, and all I'm wearing is white socks and black shoes.*

—Mario T., 44, police officer, Passaic, New Jersey

✳ ✳ ✳ ✳

My parents didn't adjust well to my being away from home. During my freshman year at college, they would find that they "just happened to be in the neighborhood" and would drop by and say hello—usually with, say, an entire round of brie. My dorm-mates loved this, because my parents would bring enough food for everyone, but the visits were excruciating. They would do this about once every other weekend. In order for them to just "happen" to be in the neighborhood, they had to drive ninety miles.

They would never call me first to warn me of their visits. But of course my social life was so lame at that point it didn't matter; there wasn't very much they could have interrupted anyway.

—Joan N., 32, journalist, New York, New York

*   *   *   *

Mom didn't want me around the house when I was sixteen, so without asking me, she signed me up for day camp—as a camper, not a counselor. Which meant that I would have guys younger than me teaching me how to weave fucking lanyards.

When I informed her I was not going, she informed me it was already paid for. We screamed about this for hours. The first day, the little yellow bus came to pick me up—you know those buses, the ones those of us who grew up in the suburbs refer to as the retard bus? Anyway, the first day, I gave in. I went.

Obviously I was as old as the counselors. I told her, "That's it. I'm not going back." She said, "You *are* going." So, basically, I hid. At 4 A.M., I moved into the attic, and I only came out of hiding when the bus left.

By this time, she was hysterical. She could only get half her money back. She refused to have me around the house.

So I went to work for my cousins, and I've been a working stiff ever since.

—Sam G., 34, advertising executive, Long Island, New York

*   *   *   *

When I was in high school, I was an almighty slob. My mother was always trying to get me to put away my clothes rather than dumping them all over my bedroom. One day, when the school bus dropped me off at my house with virtually everyone I knew on board, I saw my mother had taken *every* article of clothing I owned and scattered them over the front lawn, driveway, and the neighbor's lawn also. She saved my more personal items, like underwear and training bras, for the trees and shrubs.

—Samantha G., bartender/waitress, Little Rock, Arkansas

* * * *

My mother was a fashion maven with extraordinary powers of self-absorption; she simply couldn't believe she had given birth to two daughters whose idea of grooming was to shave their armpits on alternate Sundays.

Anyway, when we were little we had a lot of pets. One was a pedigreed beagle whom my sister had decided to enter in dog shows. Dagwood was doing very well in his division. One day, there was a particularly important show—but my sister was sick. So my mom said she would substitute.

Mom dressed to the max. How many women in Chanel suits do you see at dog shows? She literally pranced into the ring, strutting beautifully, perfect posture, eyes straight ahead, totally oblivious to what Dagwood was doing—which, as it turned out, was peeing on the judge's leg. She was so caught up in looking her best that she had forgotten to take Dagwood out for a walk before the class. The judge gave her a lecture on concentrating on the dog's presentation, but Mom was too busy concentrating on her own.

—Caterina G., 29, social worker, Berkeley, California

* * * *

I grew up in southern California, where, starting in sixth grade, just about everyone would be shipped off to summer camp for a week or more.

Anyway, I remember sitting around for mail call in a small log-built amphitheater. They began calling names to receive mail, and I remember hearing them call out a letter addressed to "Rear Admiral Dopey . . ." At this point, everyone was laughing—so was I, although I wondered what kind of sick, twisted parental mind would do that to their kid. It wasn't quite as funny when I heard the counselor reading the rest of the envelope: "Rear Admiral Dopey Ken Walden."

—Ken W., 16, high-school student, Napa, California

* * * *

What They Did for Love
(What Most Hellish Parents Are Like Underneath It All)

Your parents: the most frightening individuals on the planet. Cruel, grasping, vindictive, unpredictable, appalling. Pol Pot had nothing on these people.

Just when you think you've got them figured out, they do the unthinkable. They make you love them all over again.

* * * *

My mother, a doctor, was never much of an animal lover, but for my sake she put up with a menagerie that included dogs, cats, rabbits, gerbils, mice, tarantulas, iguanas, chameleons, parakeets, canaries, and several different kinds of snakes, including my pet boa constrictor, Julius Squeezer.

When I was very young, I had my first pet, a duck named (brilliantly) Quackers. I lived for this duck. I spent every spare minute—and a three-year-old has *lots* of spare minutes—hanging out with the duck.

One day, the duck got sick. Its feathers began to molt; it drooped, its eyes got rheumy, it stopped swimming, and it generally behaved in an unducklike manner. A couple of days went by like this. We presumed the problem was nothing more than a cold.

After a few days, Quackers went to that big pond in the sky. It happened while I was taking a nap. Panicked, my nanny called my mother, explained the situation, and stated, quite firmly, that I was too young to deal with the trauma of death. Mother agreed. She knew there was very little time to spare. With an office full of patients waiting, Mother went on the search for a replacement duck—a duck that more or less resembled Quackers. Where she found a duck in the middle of a fairly large city on such short notice, I still don't know.

Of course I don't remember this, but apparently when I woke up, I congratulated her on what a great doctor she was, with Quackers' sudden burst of health—but why did he have that black spot on his stomach?

Anyway, I discovered some years later that it wasn't only Quackers who was quickly replaced; to spare me the trauma of death, she replaced numerous gerbils, hamsters, lizards, etc., that had one paw in the grave. I was ten before she finally allowed me to know that an animal had died; at that point it was really a shock, because it seemed my animals lived forever. On the other hand, maybe that's why I've gone into the profession I have—I *wanted* to believe they could live forever.

—Stacy T., 36, veterinarian, Yonkers, New York

* * * *

When I was little (in the early fifties), I came down with the measles. My mother told me I had to drink from a "special" glass so that the other family members wouldn't catch it. She put a paper towel in "my" glass so I would know which one it was. We went somewhere after that and came back to find that the housekeeper must have misunderstood and left a paper towel in all the glasses.

My mother told me that now they were *all* my special glasses.

—Brandon M., 49, theater manager, San Francisco, California

✳   ✳   ✳   ✳

I was in the eighth grade and, once again, it was just me an' Momma. Dad had left, and we had moved into a rather large house outside of Mart, Texas, that the previous owner had died in. As the Texas autumn chilled into winter, Momma worked her two or three jobs to keep food on the table, clothes on our backs, and gas in the station wagon.

November came and it got really cold. The house was big and very hard to heat; at night it would creak and groan like the guy who had supposedly died was coming back for a visit. We only had enough warm covers for one bed. We shared a room that winter. It was getting very close to Christmas. Money was tighter than it had been in quite a while. We couldn't even afford to buy an evergreen. So we went out one gray day, and Momma found a fair-sized branch that had blown off its tree during the night. She took it into the house, used her magic (plus a little Reynolds aluminum wrap, a small jar, bits of white tablecloth and a package of gumdrops), and voilà!—instant Christmas tree. Unfortunately, we had no presents to go under it.

So the night before Christmas, Momma told me we had to leave home for a while, because Santa didn't like to be disturbed while he was working. She loaded me into the station wagon, and we drove off to her sister's house in Houston. It was a two-hundred-mile journey. I barely remember getting there; I guess I slept most of the way. We stayed only an hour and turned around to make the two-hundred-mile return trip. She tucked me back into bed when we got home.

I woke up, early as usual, and went into the living room out of habit. Sitting under our gumdrop tree, gleaming against the white tablecloth, was a handful of small, brightly wrapped boxes. To me, from Santa.

—Janet R., 30, ski instructor, Taos, New Mexico

✳   ✳   ✳   ✳

I had always breezed through school without having to work very hard, but for some reason I had a terrible time during the first half of eighth grade. I was lovesick, I couldn't pay attention, I was depressed ... all I wanted to do was sit around and read Sylvia Plath. That semester, I got my report card, and there it was: two Cs, two Ds, and an F. I didn't know how I could go home and face my parents. My life was over.

Knowing there was nothing I could do, I went home. Silently, trying hard not to tremble or break down in tears, I handed the card to my mother. She looked it over for a long, long time. "Oh, my God," she said. "Sit down. You must need a drink." And so Mom made me my first Manhattan.

I told that story when I made my valedictory speech in high school.

—Judy T., 36, English professor, Chicago, Illinois

* * * *

When there are six children in a family, sometimes little details about each kid's life get lost in the shuffle.

My baby sister was supposed to be applying for schools, but she was very, very busy. She was not only a straight-A student but also a competitive athlete involved in half a dozen extracurricular activities. Admissions were due December 31, and somewhere around December 29, Mom thought to ask her how her applications were going.

"Uh-oh," was her reply.

So that was it. Holiday activities were suspended, and we all got down to work. Each of us siblings had a different specialty, so we took different essay questions. My brother, who's an engineer, took any questions that were conceptual or mathematical; my eldest sister, who has her Ph.D. in economics, did all the economics questions; I did the creative writing (one college asked for a short story); and my mother filled in wherever she could. Basically, Molly just signed the applications.

So we were racing around, getting everything ready—it was now December 31, and things had to be postmarked by 5 P.M.

At 4:30, just before we all headed down to the post office in triumph, my mother realized that we forgot to answer one of Yale's essay questions, which went something like this: "Aliens from outer space land in your backyard. What do you want to tell them about Earth?"

My mother, in a panic, flings the application into the typewriter and quickly typed her answer on the back: "We love. Do you?" Then she threw the application into the envelope.

A few months have passed. It's April 15, D day for college admissions answers. I'm back in New York, and I call Molly. "Oh, I got into Brown," she tells me. "Great . . . but how about the others?" I asked. "Well, yeah," she replies casually, "I got into Yale, Harvard, Dartmouth, Princeton, and Columbia, too."

Incidentally, Molly also got a special note from an admissions officer at Yale: "Your answer to the question about the aliens was the best one we received, Ms. Adams."

—Emilia F., 31, magazine editor, New York, New York

✳   ✳   ✳   ✳

℗ **PLUME**

HAVE A HELL OF A LAUGH